Conscience and Caring

Creative Pastoral Care and Counseling Series
Editor: Howard J. Clinebell
Associate Editor: Howard W. Stone

Conscience and Caring

Geoffrey Peterson

Fortress Press Philadelphia

Library of Congress Cataloging in Publication Data

Peterson, Geoffrey.
  Conscience and caring.

  (Creative pastoral care and counseling series)
  Bibliography: p.
  1. Conscience.   2. Pastoral counseling.   I. Title.
II. Series.
BJ1278.C66P47   253.5   82-7401
ISBN 0-8006-0570-5   AACR2

9594C82   Printed in the United States of America   1–570

Contents

Series Foreword

Let me share with you some of the hopes that are in the minds of those of us who helped to develop this series—hopes that relate directly to you as the reader. It is our desire and expectation that these books will be of help to you in developing better working tools as a minister-counselor. We hope that they will do this by encouraging your own creativity in developing more effective methods and programs for helping people live life more fully. It is our intention in this series to affirm the many things you have going for you as a minister in helping troubled persons—the many assets and resources from your religious heritage, your role as the leader of a congregation, and your unique relationship to individuals and families throughout the life cycle. We hope to help you reaffirm the *power of the pastoral* by the use of fresh models and methods in your ministry.

The aim of the series is not to be comprehensive with respect to topics but rather to bring innovative approaches to some major types of counseling. Although the books are practice oriented, they also provide a solid foundation of theological and psychological insights. They are written primarily for ministers (and those preparing for the ministry) but we hope that they will also prove useful to other counselors who are interested in the crucial role of spiritual and value issues in all helping relationships. In addition we hope that the series will be useful in seminary courses, clergy support groups, continuing education workshops, and lay befriender training.

This is a period of rich new developments in counseling and psychotherapy. The time is ripe for a flowering of creative methods and insights in pastoral care and counseling. Our expectation is that this series will stimulate grass-roots creativity as innovative methods and programs come alive for you. Some of the major thrusts that will be discussed in this series include a new awareness of the unique contributions of the theologically trained counselor, the liberating power of the human-potentials orientation, an appreciation of the pastoral care function of the ministering congregation, the importance of humanizing systems and institutions as well as close relationships, the importance of pastoral *care* (and not just counseling), the many opportunities for caring ministries throughout the life cycle, the deep changes in male-female relationships, and the new psychotherapies such as Gestalt therapy, Transactional Analysis, educative counseling, and crisis methods. Our hope is that this series will enhance your resources for your ministry to persons by opening doorways to understanding of these creative thrusts in pastoral care and counseling.

In this volume Geoffrey Peterson focuses on understanding and helping persons with their value conflicts, ethical dilemmas, and moral hiatuses. He holds that these issues are often at the heart of the problems which bring people to counseling. I agree. This book provides on the one hand a theory and theology of conscience, and on the other an abundance of practical methods for use in counseling with persons suffering from conscience problems.

In the early stages of the modern period of pastoral care, clinically trained pastoral counselors often used their energy primarily to counteract the futile moralizing which had characterized so much pastoral care on ethical issues. They saw that such superficial moralizing had increased the unconstructive authority-centeredness and the lack of maturity in the consciences of both the helpers and helpees. In recent years many of us have become aware of the ethical context and core of pastoral care, and of human problems in living. We human beings live in our meanings, priorities, and values. Destructive, inadequate, or distorted values are involved in most personal, interpersonal, and institutional crises which motivate people to come for help. Therefore skill in helping people mature in their consciences and ethical sensitivities is a crucial skill for effective pastoral counseling and education.

The author of this book is lecturer in Pastoral Theology at the United Theological College, Sydney, Australia. His depth exploration of conscience issues has followed two complementary, interacting tracks—a theory-building track and a clinical track. Throughout his teaching ministry he has been involved in pastoral work in congregations. In recent years he also has been director of a church-related counseling center. I enjoyed getting to know Geoff and his family during the study-leave he spent in Claremont wrestling with issues of the theory and theology of conscience.

Let me share with you some of the ways I found this book to be helpful to me as a pastoral counselor. The review of five major understandings (traditional and contemporary) of the nature of conscience was illuminating. It became even more so as the author formulated a holistic, wholeness-nurturing understanding of conscience, drawing on the strengths in each of the major strands. His discussion of the dynamics of the major types of conscience problems has direct relevance to the practice of pastoral care and counseling. Persons with hair-shirt, punitive consciences need help in gaining liberation from their heavy, graceless consciences. At the other extreme, persons with underdeveloped, inactive consciences need a very different type of counseling. They need confrontational help in awakening and strengthening their ethical capacities, so they can develop more "muscle" in their concern for others. In contrast with these types of conscience problems, persons with confused, distorted consciences need help in clarifying and revising their ethical guidelines. Our contemporary society's value confusion makes this type of problem epidemic. Finally, persons with consciences burdened by self-righteousness need help in humanizing their consciences.

The book's central motif is the *transformation of consciences* so that they fulfill a creative, liberating role in ourselves and in those we seek to help. The final chapter moves far beyond the therapy of consciences to positive prevention. It spells out the process of helping ourselves and others develop more mature, healthy consciences. Here the author utilizes the rich resources of the New Testament for developing a constructive theology of conscience. He sees the total life of a worshiping, learning, serving congregation as an environment within which the consciences of members and leaders keep growing. A Christian conscience is developed and shaped by participation in the covenant community of faith.

Conscience at its best is understood as a call to wholeness. The vision of what constitutes authentic wholeness is seen in the person of Jesus Christ. The mature conscience is a liberated conscience, liberated through experiencing the love, acceptance, and forgiveness of God. A mature conscience is continually growing through the life cycle. A mature conscience is responsible—to other persons and to changing the unjust structures and oppressive institutions of our society. A mature conscience is, most of all, caring; it calls us to a global caring, a global responsibility. The caring of a mature Christian conscience is inspired and energized by a growing faith experience.

You have a potentially exciting encounter awaiting you in these pages. May this encounter be for you, as it was for me, energizing and enlivening both personally and professionally on issues of conscience.

HOWARD CLINEBELL

Preface

Ten years ago the word "conscience" had negative associations for me. It reminded me of some of the oppressive moralities I had encountered. For me, and this may be true for you too, "conscience" used to be a heavy and forbidding word. It was linked with unpleasant feelings of guilt, shame, and inadequacy, and with strict, sometimes inhuman, moral standards.

Despite these negative associations and feelings, my interest in conscience has grown steadily in recent years. In pastoral ministry I frequently met what I regarded as conscience issues or value issues. People encountering such problems often do not identify them as bound up with conscience. However, I became increasingly convinced that we can often get to the heart of a pastoral situation when we ask the key question, "What is happening here with conscience?" My brother Bruce, through his work as a psychiatrist in private practice, has reached similar conclusions. Many hours of stimulating discussion together have confirmed our common interest in this persistent theme.

Conscience issues also emerged consistently from my reading in pastoral theology and the social sciences. Partly as a result of this reading, I now believe that conscience can fulfill an affirming, constructive, and liberating role in human life. A major goal of the care and counseling described in this book is to facilitate such change in people's lives so that conscience can be experienced in this positive way, rather than as a painful and destructive force. Besides describing typical conscience problems, I want to share a vision of healthy consciences helping people to realize their potential for a fulfilling and responsible life.

Indeed, the concept of "conscience" will be used here as a basic organizing and unifying principle for pastoral care. Until recently, pastoral care often adopted a nondirective and morally neutral stance, hoping thereby to avoid imposing doctrines and values in insensitive ways. The widespread influence of Sigmund Freud and Carl Rogers encouraged this trend. Though the nondirective approach brought many gains, it may also have given the impression at times that morals and values do not matter very much. Fortunately pastoral care and counseling are currently becoming more concerned with precisely such issues. There is a growing concern in the church that the caring ministry, besides offering acceptance and understanding, should be ethically and theologically responsible. This renewed interest in values and morals may well be a sign that church communities and pastors are recovering more of the specifically pastoral dimension of their ministry.

The ideas and practices described in this book have developed through seven years of part-time parish ministry, six years of directing a church-related counseling service, and twenty years of teaching pastoral care in an Australian theological school. Most of the case studies reported here are based on situations encountered in actual counseling, with details changed to safeguard confidentiality. Most of my basic research on conscience was done during a year's study-leave in Claremont, California.

I am most grateful to the School of Theology at Claremont for that stimulating and exciting year, and to Howard Clinebell in particular for his warm interest, support, and encouragement. My warm thanks go also to Barbara, my wife, for reading and correcting the manuscript, and to Dorothy Wormald, who typed it.

1. The Pastoral Encounter with Conscience

Keith Mitchell feels deeply concerned as he struggles to find ways of helping three members of his Smithville congregation. Each of the three is caught in a complex dilemma of conscience.

The pastor thinks first of James Maxwell, whose wife died about a year ago. James still experiences tormenting guilt feelings and severe depression. Four weeks ago, in desperation, he came to Keith asking for help.

Pastor Mitchell is also thinking of Jill Kennedy, a teenager, facing a different type of conscience problem. Influenced by a group of radical college friends, Jill is questioning many of her former values, especially those relating to sexual morality. Jill feels guilty and confused, particularly at home or when she is with other members of the church youth group. Since her parents seem to her much too conservative and rigid in their attitudes on moral issues, Jill has begun to share her problem with Keith Mitchell, and also with Sarah White, one of the leaders of the Smithville youth group.

Carol Martin is also on Keith's mind. Her conscience problem is different again. Carol's husband Bill is having an affair with his office secretary. Carol has confided in the pastor, pouring out her feelings of hurt and moral indignation. She claims that Bill is unconcerned about her pain. She also feels that she is a failure as a woman, a wife, and a mother: "Without the support of the other women in the midweek Bible study group, I think I would have taken an overdose."

Pastor Mitchell is deeply concerned about these three pastoral situations, all of which center around conscience. All three of the situations involve moral standards, values, and feelings of self-worth. James Maxwell is struggling with a tormenting conscience; Jill Kennedy's conscience is confused and guilty; and Carol Martin's conscience is both outraged and ashamed. On the other hand, Carol's husband Bill has a conscience that seems to be weak or nonfunctioning in some important areas of his life; and the Kennedy parents seem to Jill to have consciences that are rigid and moralistic.

Identifying the role of conscience, the type of conscience expressing itself in each of these human situations, can help to shape effective pastoral care. Pastor Mitchell, Sarah White, and other members of the Smithville congregation are seeking ways of caring that can help the unhealthy or hurting consciences to change. Each type of conscience problem calls for a different approach. Pastoral methods that are helpful with a deeply guilty person, for example, will be different from those that are helpful with a rigid and self-righteous person. The cases of James, Jill, and Carol will be dealt with later at greater length in order to illustrate the variety of conscience problems that arise and to show some of the ways in which caring pastors can help.

Sarah White and Keith Mitchell also need some understanding of how the consciences of family members interact. The consciences of the various persons within a family inevitably influence and modify each other. If there is a significant change in the conscience of one family member, there are likely to be corresponding changes in the consciences of other family members. Teenager Jill Kennedy's troubled and uncertain conscience, for example, interacts with and is balanced by the strict and assured consciences of her parents as surely as Carol Martin's ashamed and upset conscience interacts with the apparently casual or inactive conscience of her husband Bill. Within any family the different types of conscience tend to balance and perpetuate each other. All family members usually bear some joint responsibility for what is happening with the conscience of any particular member.

James, Jill, and Carol each took the initiative in seeking help, partly because their consciences were causing them pain.

They hoped it might ease their situation if they were able to soften or calm their consciences, but they found this difficult to accomplish by themselves. Methods of caring are needed that can relieve pain and help the hurting conscience move beyond whatever is blocking its growth. For conscience to play a healthy and constructive role in human life, it needs to keep growing. A healthy conscience is not closed and static but open and dynamic. It is able to respond constructively to fresh situations that call for a reappraisal of old values and attitudes. The pastoral encounter with conscience raises key questions about the nature of conscience and about the role it can play in a healthy and fulfilled life.

What is Conscience?

What kinds of associations are aroused for you when you hear the word "conscience"? The term means different things to different people and even for the same person has varied emotional overtones when used in different contexts. Sometimes the word has moralistic associations, suggesting attitudes that are old-fashioned and oppressive; these attitudes may be linked with nagging feelings of guilt that make life miserable. In other contexts the word may recall the deep convictions of a social reformer who takes a lonely and courageous stand on an important moral issue. It is important, then, to give a brief description of the understanding of "conscience" that underlies the pastoral approach suggested here.

There is no ground for thinking of "conscience" as a specific organ or faculty within the human personality.* No internal "Jiminy Cricket" has ever been or is likely to be discovered within the human brain or nervous system. It is difficult to give a precise definition of "conscience." The term usually refers to thoughts, feelings, and actions involved in human valuing and judging. My conscience is active, for example, when I am making moral judgments about myself, other people, or society. When I am evaluating moral principles or the rights and wrongs of past and future actions, conscience is again involved. The thoughts, feelings, and actions that make up conscience can become very powerful, developing an autonomy and unity of their own. People who suffer from a tormenting conscience, for example, consistently report that for them conscience has extraordinary power and independence; they feel unable to change it.

Many different phenomena can be included within the concept of "conscience." The term can refer to feelings of approval and disapproval about past or contemplated actions, to judgments about what is right or wrong, and to strong moral convictions that lead to social action. These different phenomena, however, are often closely related to each other, as we shall see.

Sometimes I am very much aware of my conscience. At other times I am largely unaware of my conscience, but later reflection convinces me that it was far more active than I had thought at the time. The other night I kept watching a trivial film on television even though I had planned to read a serious and satisfying book. As I watched the movie, I kept trying to justify the action; I came up with convincing rationalizations, vigorously denying any guilt. Later in the evening, when I returned to my reading, I reflected about my TV watching. I realized that I had actually been inattentive and not closely followed the story in the movie. I had apparently felt more guilty than I was willing to admit at the time.

Learning theorists emphasize that the moral attitudes that are a part of conscience are learned in the same way as other attitudes.* In children moral attitudes and behavior patterns that have pleasant associations or that are in some way rewarded are likely to be repeated and strengthened. Such learning by reinforcement helps to transmit the basic values of the parents and of society to young children as they participate in the life of their family. The values of adolescents and adults are greatly influenced and sometimes changed by the expectations and practices of the friendship, vocational, recreational, religious, and interest groups to which they belong.

Social factors are of great importance in the development of conscience. The values and moral standards that form the content of conscience vary greatly from one society to another, from one family to another, and from one person to another. Until recent times, for example, it was a matter of conscience for some Eskimos to end the lives of their aged or infirm parents, a practice that would be condemned in Western society. On the other hand, these same Eskimos could not comprehend wars between villages and tribes.* Again, one person within a family may feel guilty about not attending church regularly, while another member of the same family may for various reasons feel ashamed about attending.

Since every known human society has its system of values, the experience of conscience may be regarded as universal.† An individual who seems to lack any consistent conscience is generally considered to be ill, a person in need of help. To have a conscience, then, is an essential part of what it means to be human. A constructive, growing conscience can act as a powerful, motivating force leading to responsible, fulfilling living.

Major Traditions on Conscience

Few English words have had such a confusing history as the word "conscience." The term has been used in so many different situations and cultures, with such a variety of meanings, that it may be asked whether it has any clear meaning in today's world.

Paul Tillich comments that "the history of the idea of conscience, despite the bewildering variety of interpretations that it has produced, shows some clear types and definite trends."‡ What follows is an attempt to identify and briefly describe these major traditions in terms of their historical roots and their present-day expressions. For the most part the traditions are complementary rather than contradictory. A holistic view seeks to hold the major views of conscience together, for there is indeed a great deal of overlap in what is here distinguished for purely conceptual purposes.

Guilt Feelings

Some views of conscience emphasize its judging and accusing functions. The earliest uses of the term, in popular Greek thought prior to the New Testament, convey this meaning. This view is also the dominant one in the New Testament itself, and it is doubtless the most common popular understandings of conscience today.* The judgments of conscience are generally experienced *after* an event, as when we feel guilty about something we have said or done or about something we have left undone. Freud's concept of the superego is closely related to this understanding of conscience.†

In this tradition conscience is usually described as an uncomfortable feeling, one that can become persistent and powerful. In the fourth century B.C., the Greek philosopher Demosthenes said his conscience was "paralyzing in its effects, as full of fear and trembling as the expectation of blows."‡ From the time of Demosthenes to the present day, many have described their consciences in similar terms.

Church people who have come to me for counseling sometimes report that they suffer from a painful accusing conscience. A strict, moralistic, religious upbringing can be a major factor in the development of such a conscience. Chapter 2 will consider this type of conscience in greater detail and discuss ways in which pastors and counselors can help.

Moral Guide

Another traditional view of conscience emphasizes its future orientation. Conscience is primarily concerned with value judgments and decision making; it is a guide for daily living. Our consciences direct us to right moral paths. The classical expression of this tradition is found in Thomas Aquinas, who in the thirteenth century understood conscience as the activity of the human reason when making moral judgments or value choices.§

This second tradition emphasizes thinking and reasoning processes rather than feelings. In Freudian terms, the focus is on ego morality rather than on the activities of the superego. Jean Piaget and Lawrence Kohlberg, using the results of extensive research, have sketched a comprehensive picture of the thinking processes involved in conscience development from childhood to adulthood.‖ Their theories of moral development point to a series of stages through which an individual passes in growing toward moral maturity. We shall return to these theories in chapter 3, for they are a helpful resource for moral education with children and adolescents and for counseling with people facing moral problems.

Pastors are often asked for guidance by people who are confused about moral issues. A woman in her early twenties recently wanted to discuss with me the rights and wrongs of homosexual behavior. She was considering whether it would be morally right for her, a believing Christian, to become "gay." In several sessions we discussed in a rational manner the biblical materials touching on homosexuality as well as relevant insights from the social sciences. Our discussions fostered positive conscience development for both of us, where "conscience" is understood primarily in relation to the process of making moral judgments.

A Form of Self-Awareness

A third cluster of views on conscience recognizes the close links between "conscience" and "consciousness" and places the main emphasis on self-awareness. Theologian John Macquarrie, for example, says that "conscience can be understood as a special and very fundamental mode of self-awareness, the awareness of 'how it is with oneself.' "* It is because we humans have the capacity for reflecting on our experience that the concept of conscience becomes possible. Conscience includes our awareness of the gap between our actual self and the self we would like to be or feel called to be.

This third tradition is closely linked to the first. The emphasis here, however, is on present experience and on a person's existing self-image rather than on events of the past. The dominant negative feeling described by this tradition is usually one of inadequacy or unworthiness rather than guilt.

There is often an inner dialogue involved in conscience, with one voice accusing and the other voice excusing or defending. Counselors sometimes encourage those being counseled to pursue this inner dialogue of conscience, so that they can experience both sides of the dialogue more keenly and move towards a resolution of any conflict.

Macquarrie's definition, as he himself says, deals with only one level of conscience. Other levels of conscience can remain hidden from awareness for long periods of time, perhaps expressing themselves only in the symbolic form of dreams and fantasies until such time as they are brought into consciousness by some unusual event. As we shall see, dreams sometimes express unconscious dimensions of conscience.

A Social Phenomenon

Another important tradition claims that conscience is essentially a social phenomenon. Social theories of conscience generally claim that conscience is primarily the process by which we internalize the predominant values of our society.* The social nature of conscience is expressed by the word itself, for the literal meaning (from the Latin *con* + *scientia*) *is* "knowledge with" or "shared knowledge." The knowledge of ourselves that is involved in conscience comes largely through our relationships with others and through our participation in various meaningful groups.

One of the most influential representatives of this tradition, the French sociologist Emile Durkheim, regarded society as the only source of values, determining both conduct and the individual conscience. He believed that it is valid to talk in terms of a group conscience, especially when a group or society becomes cohesive, having its own internal norms.†

I do not accept Durkheim's view that society is the *only* source of values. Nevertheless I believe that pastors need to recognize the powerful influence that group values have in forming and changing individual consciences. When a person has a sense of belonging in two or more groups having very different values, a conflict of conscience processes is almost inevitable. Pastors and counselors need the insights and skills that will enable them to help people clarify their divergent values and resolve such moral conflicts.

The Call to be Truly Human

A fifth and final tradition on conscience highlights what a constructive conscience can become when human life is at its best. Philosophers and theologians influenced by existentialist thought have particularly emphasized this approach. They present conscience as an inner call to realize our potentialities for creative living, to use our gifts and powers in constructive caring and responsible action.

Both Martin Heidegger and Martin Buber speak of conscience as "a call."*They agree that conscience has a negative dimension: it makes us aware of the inauthentic nature of much of our everyday living. But conscience also prods and calls us towards a more genuine expression of our humanity: it calls us "to care." For Buber this authentic living to which we are called is essentially a life of dialogue, a life in community, in which we respect and value each other as persons. Unfortunately this creative call of conscience is often silenced by pressures to conform to the expectations of others and by the functioning of immature consciences.

From a Christian point of view it may be said that an important part of the church's mission is to help all members of Christ's people hear and respond to this call of the authentic positive conscience. God's call to discipleship can be heard in and through the call of such a conscience. On the other hand, we cannot lightly or directly identify the call of conscience with God's call, since our own feelings, prejudices, and needs inevitably affect the way in which we experience conscience.

This last tradition on conscience draws upon the other traditions and brings them into close relationship with each other. It recognizes within the activities of conscience the roles of guilt, moral judgment, self-awareness, and social concern. The emphasis, however, is on the creative call to us humans to be caring and responsible persons. A holistic approach to conscience integrates the other traditions around this fifth tradition.

An awareness of these five overlapping traditions of conscience helps us as pastors to identify various dimensions of the operation of conscience. An important goal for our pastoral ministry is to facilitate the transformation of conscience so that it fulfills a constructive and liberating role both in ourselves and in those whom we are seeking to help. The holistic approach opens up possibilities for understanding and experiencing conscience in new and more constructive ways.

Voice of God or Device of the Devil?

People who come for pastoral counseling rarely see conscience as constructive. They usually report that, for them, conscience is painful and unhelpful. They also report that the dictates of conscience often have great authority, bringing a strong sense of "ought." This raises the question, "What authority should we give to the messages of conscience?"

In popular thought conscience is often equated wth the voice of God within us. There is some historical basis for this point of view. Influential philosophers of the eighteenth and nineteenth centuries, including Rousseau and Cardinal Newman, described conscience as divine and infallible.* Their influence lives on. The view that conscience never errs can be associated with each of the five traditions described in the previous section. Most scholars today, however, strongly argue that both individual conscience and group consciences can be wrong in their judgments.† To support their argument they often refer to sociological studies that have demonstrated a close relationship between conscience and culture.

Some of the greatest crimes against humanity have been committed in the name of "conscience." Nazi leaders, including Adolph Eichmann, claimed that they were following conscience when they tried to exterminate the Jews. Jewish and Roman authorities were following their group consciences when they sent Christ to the cross. Likewise church leaders were following their consciences when they burned "heretics" at the stake. In wars that destroyed countless lives both sides fought "with a good conscience."

The human conscience can be cruel, deceptive, confused, weak, self-righteous, and divisive. The pastoral situations Keith Mitchell encountered at his Smithville parish reveal conscience acting in misleading and destructive ways. The New Testament supports this realistic view of conscience. It mentions the "weak" conscience (1 Cor. 8:7) and the "evil" conscience (Heb. 10:22) as well as the "good" conscience (1 Tim. 1:19). It speaks of the need for guilty consciences to be "cleansed" and "purified" through the forgiveness offered in Jesus Christ (Heb. 9:14; 10:22). Paul insists that possession of a "clear" conscience does not necessarily mean innocence; the Lord, says Paul, is the only authoritative judge of our innocence or guilt (1 Cor. 4:4).

Whether a person's conscience accuses or affirms, then, it can be in error. The conscience which either judges or commends us is itself under the judgment of God. Popular wisdom, like a popular song of some time ago, may counsel, "Always let your conscience be your guide," but the Bible does not encourage such a blind trust in conscience. Our "Jiminy Crickets" are open to bribes and to persuasive inner manipulation. The human conscience is as much in need of the Spirit's cleansing and renewal as any other dimension of our lives. And this process of renewal must be a continuing one if conscience is to convey God's truth to us.

This has important implications for pastoral care. The functioning of conscience carries a sense of divine authority for many people, especially for those with a strict religious upbringing. Therefore the message conscience brings about the self is often accepted without question, even when the message is false and damaging. Sometimes, then, supportive pastors need to encourage people to confront and challenge the distorted messages being given by their consciences. Pastors can seek ways and means of helping people break the power of a destructive conscience.

Conscience in some people needs softening and humanizing; in others it needs awakening and strengthening and in still others it needs clarifying and renewing. Our consciences need to be tested by criteria drawn mainly from Christ's life and teachings, and then challenged to change. Part of the purpose of the Smithville congregation's pastoral ministry is to provide a quality of caring and counseling that will facilitate change towards more constructive and holistic consciences.

2. The Tormenting Conscience

Though Western society during this century has become increasingly permissive, there are still many people, both within the church and without, who suffer deeply from a tormenting conscience. In a small sharing group I led recently, one participant had just been through a divorce. He spoke of his conscience as "a hammer in the head, incessantly pounding," and he insisted that this was no mere figure of speech—he was feeling the hammer at that moment! Some of those who come to me for counseling report that they now find it impossible to attend church, even though they are believing Christians; they simply experience too much fear, depression, and guilt in the worship services, especially during the preaching. For them, just thinking or talking about a church service can arouse anxiety and guilt.

Negative Conscience

Most of us probably experience negative conscience in a much less severe form. Nevertheless we are aware of its activity in our lives. Many people identify conscience exclusively with such accusing guilt feelings. They seem to be unaware of the other major traditions on conscience described in chapter 1. Norman Bull, an English researcher on moral development, carried out an extensive survey on the moral attitudes of children and adolescents. He found that of the participants who referred to conscience all without exception spoke of the negative, punitive kind of conscience. Seventeen-year-olds, for example, used such phrases as "Conscience plays on your mind,"

"It bugs you all the time," "You can't sleep, you feel rotten."* When conscience is identified with nagging guilt feelings, it is likely to be seen as a major enemy of human happiness and fulfillment.

Guilt and Shame

With some people the tormenting conscience brings feelings of guilt, but with others the dominant feeling is more one of shame. Though guilt and shame should not be sharply separated from each other, they are associated with different kinds of human experience. Guilt is generally associated with an awareness of having done wrong, of having violated some rule or law. Shame is linked more with a sense of inadequacy, of failing to reach a standard, and with the experience or fear of being exposed. Helen Lynd sees shame as an experience of the total self, linked with one's self-image, whereas guilt is usually oriented towards particular acts of wrongdoing.† She thus links experiences of shame with the struggle for identity, one of the key struggles in Western society.

A society which has become permissive about rules and moral standards, but which also emphasizes achievement and performance, is likely to foster shame more than guilt. Some scholars claim that Western society has shifted from being dominantly guilt-oriented to being largely shame-oriented.‡ And it is often the high achievers who feel most ashamed, especially if they are "one hundred percenters" who are never satisfied with their performance.

On the other hand, it is also true that in a permissive society painful guilt feelings are often disowned or denied. We become quite adept at finding subtle ways of concealing our guilt feelings from ourselves. We are often unaware that we are doing this. And concealed guilt can cause more difficulties in our lives than acknowledged guilt. Guilt feelings that have been dormant for years, for example, can be triggered by a later crisis, such as acute grief. At a deep level we may not be as free from guilt as we think.

Most experiences of a persistent, punitive conscience include both guilt and shame. And both are usually associated with feelings of failure, inadequacy, and low self-esteem.

Persistent Depression

When James Maxwell's wife died suddenly at the age of fifty-five, many friends in the Smithville congregation marvelled at James's courage. For the first few months he maintained his customary courteous and cheerful manner. He appeared to be keeping his emotions under tight control. Even his pastor agreed at first that James seemed to be coping well. As the months went by, however, Keith Mitchell began to wonder. James was becoming more quiet and withdrawn. The one daughter still at home remarked to several friends that she was worried about her father. Pastor Mitchell invited James to talk matters over but James insisted, "No, everything's fine!"

Eventually, almost a year after his wife's death, a tense and nervous James Maxwell rang the pastor and asked if he could come and talk. In the interview that followed, James admitted to Keith, after much hesitation and struggle, that he had been feeling acutely depressed for some time. As Keith listened with warmth and understanding, James began to express his feelings more freely. "God must have abandoned me," he cried. "But I suppose I can't blame him. I've been a worthless creature."

"How is it that you have such a low opinion of yourself," Keith asked, "when others, like myself, have so much respect for you?"

James told Keith that he had often been tense and irritable with his wife; on one occasion he had verbally attacked her and then pushed her into a chair. After James had poured out his feelings about this incident, Keith invited him to share with God his sense of failure. Following a prayer of confession the pastor affirmed God's forgiveness, placing his hands on James's head as he did so.

For a few days after this confession, James felt some relief. A week later, however, on his next visit to Keith, he reported that the guilt and depression had returned. This time James confessed that he had become very angry in a heated argument with his daughter. On his next visit to the pastor James confessed to some mildly dishonest business practices in the distant past. On each visit there was one major confession to make; and on each occasion, Keith affirmed God's forgiveness. Following each confession, James always felt some initial relief from his guilt and depression, but the relief was short-lived.

Keith noticed that James's sense of guilt often seemed out of proportion to the seriousness of his "crimes." James was constantly analyzing both past events in his life and his ongoing relationships with God and other people. Keith gained the impression that James's quest for guilt and his feelings of guilt were fulfilling a deep need, that James might be lost without them. Keith wondered, "Should I suggest referral to a psychiatrist?"

The pastor decided that before raising the possibility of referral he would try to change his counseling approach. He first talked with James about some of the ways in which conscience becomes negative and destructive. "Such a conscience should not be identified with the word of God," Keith explained. "A healthy conscience affirms us rather than consistently condemning us."

Keith then encouraged James to express some of his angry feelings about his conscience. He invited James to imagine that his conscience was sitting there in the empty chair beside him, and to express what he was feeling towards the conscience that was tormenting him so much. That done, James moved to the empty chair himself and *became* that very conscience, responding himself to what he had just said to the empty chair. The process continued for some minutes, with the roles—and chairs—being switched regularly. In this way deeper feelings about conscience were aroused. When James later discussed the experience with Keith, he reported that he was beginning to understand the way conscience was operating in his life. James also reported that he was gaining a little more control over his tormenting guilt feelings.

Keith also taught James some simple methods of relaxation,

using progressive muscle relaxation, breathing exercises, and fantasies of relaxing scenes, as on a beach or by a mountain stream.* He invited James through fantasy to return to scenes from his childhood and to experience them again as though he were a little boy.

In one such fantasy the pastor invited James to imagine a scene from his childhood in which he was upset and unhappy. James spent some minutes silently recalling and reliving a certain incident. After the fantasy exercise James, with considerable emotion, said, "That was terribly painful! I'm not sure that I want to talk about it." After another period of silence, he began to sob.

When the sobbing finally subsided James began to speak, slowly, hesitantly: "I was just five years old . . . I saw my mother and father quarreling bitterly . . . my mother was threatening to leave home . . . my father had accused her of having another man as a lover . . . my mother accused him of deliberately lying to hurt her . . . she was almost hysterical. I thought I had put that scene out of my mind." James went on to describe how his mother had then left the family for about four months to live on her own. She later returned and a partial reconciliation with her husband took place. James said that his father was strict and rigid in his moral standards and did not easily relent. The situation remained tense for many months.

"Putting myself back into that scene," said James, "I felt a mixture of fear, anger, and guilt. I felt guilty because I was convinced that the trouble in the family was largely my fault. As a boy I had often been difficult and stubborn, and that used to upset my Mom so much. She really did care for us all—even me!" More sobbing. More silence.

By the end of the session James was emotionally exhausted. At the same time, however, he was beginning to feel some lightness and hope. The pastor had helped him to see how his strong but confused feelings towards his mother and his fear of his father had continued to play an important role in his adult life, affecting even his relationship with his wife. The sudden death of his wife had reawakened those old feelings of loss, fear, anger, and guilt. James said that he had gained in self-understanding and was increasingly able to accept himself as he is. When he made his confession to God at the end of this session, James gratefully accepted God's forgiveness and love. He returned home with a quiet yet deep sense of liberation.

The relief from depression and guilt, though not permanent, was this time of longer duration. Keith encouraged James to be more open and communicative, especially with his daughter and with some of his faithful friends in the Smithville congregation. James was able to share with two of these friends some of the things that he had previously confessed only to Keith. The depression was still there at times, especially in the mornings, but it was much less severe. James felt he could now cope with life, given the support of Pastor Mitchell and the Smithville congregation, and the assurance that the future was in the hands of a loving and forgiving God.

The Superego Conscience

Freud's theories about the development of the superego give some helpful clues for understanding the processes involved in a tormenting conscience. Freud pointed out that the human ego can observe and criticize itself. These functions of the ego can thus be separated from other functions. Freud introduced the term "superego" to denote this watching, judging function (the prefix "super" means "above"). Freud goes on to say that "the superego has the ego at its mercy and applies the most severe moral standards to it."*

For the developing child the process of identification, especially with the parent of the same sex, plays a most important role in superego development. Children four or five years old increasingly internalize parental standards and prohibitions. Even when the parents are not physically present, children can feel guilty if their behavior does not conform to parental standards. Conscience is then acting as an inner parent. Freud believed that these superego conscience processes are nonrational and act mainly at an unconscious level.

When a punitive, internalized parent figure persists into later adulthood, it becomes resistant to change. James Maxwell's fear of his father doubtless played an important role in the development of his tormenting conscience. It seemed to James, with his particular religious upbringing, that God was angrily punishing him for his past failures. James felt that he was utterly unworthy of God's love. His deeper feelings about his father were mixed with his feelings towards God.

Freud found that even if a child's parents are gentle and kind, the superego dimensions of conscience may still be accusing and harsh.* He maintained that aggression and anger, when blocked from outward expression, for whatever reason turn inwards against the self, linking with conscience processes and making them more punitive. The internalized parent is often much harsher than the real parent. Indeed it is precisely the child of benevolent parents with high ideals who feels least able to express aggression outwardly. The anger simply builds and festers within. This points up the importance of our accepting anger as a part of human life and of developing ways to deal with it constructively.†

Destructive and Creative Guilt

In James Maxwell's life destructive guilt feelings were robbing him of self-esteem and hope in the future. They tended to poison his relationships with others by arousing fear and suspicion. They also deprived him of confidence, thereby sabotaging his efforts to do something constructive about his problem. At the height of his crisis, the guilt feelings snowballed. James's experience was accurately described centuries earlier by Martin Luther, who also suffered from a tormenting conscience: "From one sin for which we feel we are being punished we imagine countless other sins."‡ Luther knew from experience that guilt can become increasingly destructive.

Not all guilt feelings, however, are destructive. When we act in uncaring or irresponsible ways, it is appropriate to feel guilty about our actions. Appropriate guilt feelings can act as helpful danger signals, indicating that something is not right, that our priorities are wrong, that someone is being hurt. They may also embody a constructive longing for forgiveness and reconciliation. Guilt feelings of this kind should be acknowledged and acted upon as soon as possible. As the feelings are usually painful, the temptation of course is to deny them. But guilt that is evaded or denied is likely to bring eventual trouble and conflict. Guilt feelings can be appropriate and helpful.

Feelings of guilt should be distinguished from real or objective guilt. A person who feels guilty is not necessarily culpable of wrongdoing. A child may feel very guilty when a parent dies, even though the child may in no way have been responsible for the parent's death. On the other hand, a person may commit a major crime, yet show no sign of guilt. Sometimes we pastors can help people soften and control inappropriate guilt feelings. At other times people need support to enable them to face real guilt and deal with it constructively.

Healthy and unhealthy guilt feelings are often tangled together. They can be difficult to separate. Such separation may require the help of an understanding pastor or counselor. Pastors can facilitate the process of distinguishing inappropriate from appropriate guilt feelings. James Maxwell's pastor helped him see that some of his guilt feelings were inappropriate—out of proportion to the seriousness of the "crime" that triggered them. Inappropriate guilt feelings sometimes result when unacknowledged guilt, separated from the situation that was its source, is attached instead to some other event not nearly as serious. There is something wrong, for example, if I feel guilty about forgetting one item on a shopping trip but am unworried about being rude and hurtful to my wife.

An inappropriate degree of self-rejection or self-hatred can be one indication of unhealthy guilt feelings. People plagued by this "neurotic guilt" may try to alleviate it by various forms of self-punishment. They may behave in such a way as to elicit punishment from the environment. They may marry spouses who are abusive and cruel. They may be especially prone to accidents, injuries, or disasters. They may develop physical symptoms, such as headaches, backaches, abdominal pains, or skin ailments. They may use alcohol or drugs destructively. They can tolerate themselves better when they are suffering misfortune than when things are going well for them. On the other hand, because of their need to keep atoning for their guilt, they may find it hard to accept compliments, gifts, success, or good fortune.

Symptoms and behavior patterns of the kind here described express the internal need for a deserved punishment that can pacify the stern and angry conscience. Such symptoms may bring temporary relief. In the long run, however, self-punishing behavior tends only to make matters worse, bringing an even greater sense of hopelessness. The symptoms may be understood as attempts at self-justification, as efforts to earn pity, approval, and love from self, others, and God. They may gain some sympathy, but the honest and loving acceptance and self-forgiveness that satisfy our deepest human needs cannot be bought in this way. Such acceptance is received only as a gift within a relationship of trust.

Confession

The church throughout its history has sought to bring relief and renewal to people suffering from a tormenting conscience. The gospel has at its heart the good news of God's acceptance of confessing, believing sinners, and of God's readiness and power to forgive and renew. Confession and the experience of God's forgiveness, mediated through the church, have for many centuries brought liberation and joy to believers.

The practice of confessing to another person has not been confined to the church. It was practiced by many ancient societies in a variety of contexts, including the early ancestors of the native Americans. It can also occur within a modern medical context. Karl Menninger tells of a patient who had been a cardiac invalid, living in constant fear of recurring anginal seizures. Eventually the patient reluctantly confessed that he had for a long time been experiencing homosexual temptations. He had been terrified that he might yield to these temptations and be condemned. Following confessions and a rational discussion of his problem, "the heart symptoms almost entirely disappeared."*

Broadened Understandings

Change may be needed in some of the traditional ways of practicing confession in the church. In the past the confessor has sometimes been regarded as a superior spiritual "father," hearing and directing a troubled person or "child."† Confession is then a one-way process. In our kind of society a greater degree of mutuality is desirable. Sensitive confessors and counselors are ready, when appropriate, to be vulnerable and open about their own weaknesses.

There is also a need to broaden the scope of confession as it has often been conceived and practiced. Confession can be interpreted in the general sense of a sharing with trusted others "how it is with one's self." This certainly includes the sharing of failures, wrongdoings, and shortcomings, but it may also include a sharing of hopes, desires, and beliefs, and even successes and strengths. The act of confessing one's faith is encompassed by such a broadened understanding of confession. It involves confessing who we are and what we believe and value. Making use of John Macquarrie's definition of conscience as "the awareness of how it is with one's self,"‡ confession can be understood as the sharing of one's conscience, including both its positive and negative dimensions.

Accurate identification and sharing of one's feelings is an important part of confession. To share myself with another, I need to be aware of what is happening within me and between us. This kind of awareness does not come easily. We humans learn many ways of concealing parts of ourselves, especially the sensitive, hurting parts. If a pastor or counselor is in touch with the deeper feeling dimensions of a relationship, facilitation of this kind of awareness and sharing is more likely to take place. Some of the awareness exercises described in the next section can be helpful in this facilitation process. They can be used in both individual and group contexts.

According to the so-called "paradoxical theory of change,"

growth in self-awareness is likely to bring constructive changes in behavior.* The theory claims that changes in our behavior do not usually come as a result of our anxious striving or of the efforts of others to change us. Anxious striving often brings frustration and greater impotence. Coercion tends to produce resistance to change. On the other hand, increased self-awareness followed by confession within an accepting relationship prepares the way for constructive change. A skilled and understanding counselor can facilitate both the confession and the resulting changes in behavior.

A straightforward confession to a pastor or fellow Christian, however, does not usually overcome neurotic or inappropriate guilt. James Maxwell could have continued to confess endlessly to Keith Mitchell, without experiencing genuine liberation. His guilt was rooted in conflicts of which he was largely unaware. Repeated confessing did not deal with these deep inner conflicts. Guilt which has been denied or evaded cannot be confessed until the person is aware of the guilt and able to face it. And where guilt feelings have been displaced from a primary situation to a secondary situation, confession related exclusively to the secondary situation does not help. Regular confession can become a way of appeasing rather than overcoming neurotic guilt feelings. As in James Maxwell's case, what is needed are methods of helping that can foster the awareness and working through of the deeper feelings and conflicts. Some confrontation may also be needed to challenge the person to change habitual ways of dealing with disturbing feelings. A challenge to relate more openly with others may help the person conquer tendencies towards brooding over problems. A pastor or other helper who does not have sufficient time or training to deal effectively with situations involving these deeper levels of guilt should refer such persons to a trained psychotherapist or pastoral counseling specialist.†

Helping Confession to Happen

Effective confession involves more than thinking and talking. Accompanying the verbal expression there needs to be a genuine expression of feeling. Pastoral counselors and other helpers should have ways of encouraging guilt-laden persons to go beyond mere verbalizing and intellectualizing.

If a counseling relationship with good rapport has been established, some of the methods described below for fostering awareness of partly concealed feelings may help to trigger effective confession. Following the example of Keith Mitchell, we may invite a person to imagine his or her tormenting conscience occupying an empty chair and then to express their feelings towards that conscience. That done, the person then occupies the previously vacant chair, *becomes* that very conscience, and responds to what has just been said. As in the case of James Maxwell, there is a repeated switching of roles. The imagined occupant of the empty chair could also be a parent, or God.

People may also be invited to close their eyes and relax, and to imagine that they are looking at themselves in a mirror. They are invited to be critical of the image they see (this exercise is usually more helpful if the criticisms are expressed audibly). They then respond to these same criticisms, as if they are the figure in the mirror speaking back. The process continues, with the roles being switched repeatedly.* This exercise can trigger a dialogue of conscience between the superego and ego. It can lead to a helpful sharing with the counselor in the debriefing which follows.

A similar fantasy exercise, which Pastor Mitchell also used with James Maxwell, goes like this:

> Close your eyes and relax; recall some past situation in which you felt guilty or ashamed, perhaps as a child or a teenager; recall the surroundings and the people who were present; recall what you were doing and saying, and what others were doing and saying; put yourself back into the situation as if it were happening now; be in touch with the feelings involved; stay with the scene for a few minutes; when you are ready, open your eyes and return to the room where we are now.

The counselee then describes the experience in the first person and the present tense. In the subsequent debriefing, there is encouragement to express and explore the feelings that have been generated.

Gestures, nonverbal symbolic acts, and simple rituals can foster the accepting and experiencing of God's forgiveness. As an act of identification I sometimes hold a person's hand during a confession, whether that confession is being made to me as a representative of the church or directly to God in prayer. If there are no obvious risks involved, I may place my hands on a person's head or shoulders when affirming God's forgiveness. On occasion the confession is written out on paper, and the paper is then torn into small pieces or burned, its destruction symbolizing our faith that the offending attitudes and actions have been forgiven by God. I usually try to explore in advance the question of what actions are likely to be most helpful for the persons involved by suggesting alternative possibilities and inviting their response.

Following Up

Confession to a third party may not of itself accomplish a great deal. The person confessing may subsequently repeat the offensive behavior, knowing that now there is a way of gaining relief from whatever guilt may develop. Relief gained through confession, however, should lead to a more open and responsible kind of behavior.

Pastors can mention to people making confession two or three steps that could be taken by way of follow-up. First, it may be helpful to share at least some parts of the confession with one or two "significant others." A married person, for example, may need to be more open with a spouse; a teenager may need to share with a parent, or vice versa; a single person may need to confide in a close friend. If the person making confession is associated with a small sharing group or growth group in which a considerable degree of trust has already been developed, a second possibility can be explored, that of sharing part of the confession with that group.

A wise pastor will approach these possibilities with sensitivity and tact. It is not necessarily constructive for spouses, for example, to share with each other previous sexual indiscretions. Total "honesty" can destroy some marriages. A hasty or premature confession, while it may reduce one's own guilt feelings, can at the same time cause enormous pain to the person to whom one is confessing! Damaged marriage relationships need to be rebuilt and trust restored before a complete confession can be constructive. A tactful confession, however, should result in a growing openness within the marital relationship and an increased readiness to share weaknesses as well as strengths.

Finally, it may be productive to explore with people making confession the possibility of expressing their new-found forgiveness and liberation in concrete and practical ways. Some may wish to make restitution for the wrongs and hurts they have done. Some may seek opportunities to help other people battling similar problems. It is important that such actions be the outworking of gratitude for forgiveness rather than an attempt to earn approval or atone for guilt.

Positive Conscience

Catholic theologian John Glaser tells of a married man, with several children, who had been plagued by masturbation for fifteen years. Weekly confession and communion had not helped. In counseling, the man was helped to question the authority of his punitive conscience, so that he did not judge himself so harshly. Masturbation was no longer viewed as such a serious sin. Encouraged by the counselor, the man reduced his attendance at confession to once every six weeks. The counselor then challenged him to hear the call of positive conscience to greater sexual maturity and to more caring relationships with his wife and children, to respecting them as persons. "Within several months," Glaser reports, "this fifteen-year-old 'plague' simply vanished from his life."* When the man heard and responded to the call that comes through positive conscience the power of his punitive conscience was finally broken.

Important principles emerge from reflection on such pastoral situations. First, the Glaser case shows how the church has sometimes bolstered the tormenting conscience by its legalistic and judgmental attitudes towards such widespread practices as masturbation.* Second, the case illustrates that in counseling it can sometimes be helpful to engage in a tactful debunking of a tormenting conscience, questioning both its authority and the soundness of its judgments: Christians need to be reminded that their true judge is not the conscience—which can be both cruel and false—but the most human and understanding Person who ever lived.

Glaser's case also illustrates that one of the most effective ways of dealing with a punitive conscience is to foster the development of a constructive positive conscience. Such a conscience can become an effective motivating force in a person's life. The problems focused by the punitive conscience should not be ignored or treated lightly. However, directing all of one's energies into the effort to eradicate or soften such a conscience can be self-defeating.

Most professionals, building on Freud's theory of the superego conscience, have attached greater importance to the constructive role of a positive conscience. Erik Erikson recognizes the role of the primitive, superego conscience, but views it as "a makeshift developmental mechanism" that for adequate moral development needs to be superseded by more rational, positive, and flexible conscience processes.† In a similar way, Erich Fromm distinguishes between what he calls the "authoritarian conscience," which is the voice of internalized authority, and the "humanistic conscience," which is an expression of the true self. This humanistic conscience calls us to use our gifts and power in productive and caring ways.‡ Fromm's understanding of conscience is very helpful; indeed his "humanistic conscience" corresponds to what I have called the constructive positive conscience, though I would give more recognition than he does to the actions of the grace of God in strengthening and renewing our consciences.

A major goal in counseling is to facilitate the transformation of a punitive conscience so that it becomes more constructive. Strengthening the positive conscience can sometimes help to break the power of a punitive conscience. In the case described by John Glaser the critical moment of growth came when the man was able to shift the focus of his attention away from his masturbation problem and toward the call for responsible adulthood.

People with punitive consciences are often preoccupied with God's judgments; they tend to see God as stern and forbidding. People with strong positive consciences, on the other hand, are more likely to emphasize God's understanding and love. Our faith in God's goodness and love can be of crucial importance in helping us to hear and respond to the call of a constructive positive conscience. We pastoral counselors seek to facilitate growth in faith, both through the quality of our counseling relationship and by being open and honest about our own faith. Appropriate, sensitive self-disclosure can fulfill an important role in effective counseling.*

We pastors should also be aware of the important influence of our own consciences. Persons suffering from a tormenting conscience often identify with and to some degree internalize the values and conscience processes of their counselor—ideally more positive than punitive. This process of identification can fulfill an important role in healing. Therefore we pastors and counselors should regularly examine our own consciences, which need continuing challenge and call to be increasingly constructive, responsible, and caring. Regular participation in an accepting growth group, in which honest feedback is constantly given and received, can help to keep a pastor's conscience growing. Regular confession, followed by a trustful receiving of the gospel word of forgiveness and affirmation, helps to keep the punitive conscience from gaining power.

3. Weak and Underdeveloped Consciences

The worried parents of fifteen-year-old Alec Brown brought their son to Pastor David Carrington, a specialist in pastoral counseling. Alec had repeatedly been in trouble with the police, mainly for stealing cars. Because of persistent behavior problems and frequent absenteeism he had some time ago been asked to leave school. Since leaving, he had not stayed with any job for more than a few months. He would frequently be absent from work for days at a time, going off with a gang of friends who became involved in stealing more cars. He often stayed away from home as many as four or five days at a time. The Browns complained that Alec seemed to have no conscience or remorse about his crimes, or about the worry he was causing his parents. When he was at home, Alec was quiet, said to be uncommunicative and passively resistant.

Mr. and Mrs. Brown were faithful church people, in attendance every week. From childhood Alec had himself attended both church and Sunday school. He even joined the church youth group, but then left after a few months, declaring that he had no friends there. Alec was the fourth child in a family of six brothers and one sister. The eldest son was married and no longer lived at home. Alec's mother and father both worked to support their large family.

Pastor Carrington noted that Alec was very short for his age, looking more like twelve or thirteen than fifteen years old. At first he saw Alec alone on several occasions, endeavoring to build a friendly relationship with him. On other occasions he saw Alec with his parents. David found that Alec had become part of a teenage gang while he was still at school. Alec had status in the gang, mainly because he was the quickest and smoothest at breaking into a car. Alec was clearly proud of this accomplishment, and he shared his pride with the pastor.

Inactive Conscience

Since Alec expressed little if any guilt about his dishonesty and stealing, or about the hurt he was bringing to his family, we may conclude that his conscience was relatively inactive. To describe it in this way is not to judge Alec as a person. His apparent moral indifference could be only a front, an outward way of concealing deep inner feelings that he is unable or unwilling to express.

Actually, there are two types of inactive conscience. Though related, they are very different. Both occur frequently today. First, there is the underdeveloped conscience, the conscience that has never become an effective force in a person's life. This may be the result of severe emotional deprivation in childhood. Second, there is the conscience that is well developed in some areas of life but still has significant "gaps." Alec, for example, seemed reasonably responsible in many other areas of life but apparently had no conscience about his stealing.

Both these types of conscience can be profoundly affected if a person belongs to a socially deviant group, such as a youth gang. In most gangs there is strong pressure on the members to conform to the values of the peer group. These values usually deviate widely from those commonly accepted by the community at large. If they have not learned them previously, gang members soon learn unconventional attitudes and antisocial values. They feel guilt if they break the deviant rules and values of the gang. Groups displaying aggressive, destructive behavior, uninhibited by guilt or shame, are common in today's urban culture.

David Carrington's goal in working with Alec was to help his conscience become stronger, more caring, and more responsible than it had been. The pastor took into account the important influence of the gang and the fact of Alec's mixed relationships with other members of his family.

The problems experienced by Alec Brown and his family are

symptomatic of our time. Behavior and character disorders of various kinds are extremely widespread. While Freud pointed to the unhappiness and suffering caused by the oppressive conscience, today the opposite problem seems at least equally common: many consciences are inactive, weak, or underdeveloped. Of all the conscience problems discussed in this book, this type is probably the most difficult to deal with effectively.

Conscience Counseling

Pastor Carrington's individual sessions with Alec were fairly informal, intended mainly to build a good relationship. They were followed by several joint counseling sessions at which the parents and Alec were present together. Several interviews were held in the Browns' home, with the youngest member of the family, eleven-year-old Richard, also present. Other members of the family were not willing to participate in the counseling. One older brother seemed to be particularly aggressive and bitter towards Alec.

In the individual sessions it became clear that Alec's needs for recognition and status were not being met in the home. Mr. Brown tended to be distant and cold and was a strict disciplinarian. Alec said he had never been able to talk freely with his father. Alec's mother was warmer toward him but she was always busy. She also tended to be perpetually anxious. It was clear that in his gang Alec was enjoying a status and sense of belonging that he had never experienced at home.

In the joint sessions with Alec and his parents some helpful confrontation took place on both sides, under David's watchful supervision. Encouraged by the pastor, Alec told his parents why he was never happy at home. Mr. and Mrs. Brown became aware of Alec's needs for recognition and status. They began to appreciate that as long as Alec gained his sense of belonging from the gang, rather than from his family, he was going to be strongly influenced by the values of the gang. They also gained an understanding of the social processes that produce antisocial gangs. On their side, the parents told Alec that, besides violating the rights of others, he was grieving and hurting his own parents by his lying and stealing. They admitted that they were finding it difficult to cope with the situation. Pastor Carrington supported the parents as they confronted Alec with moral issues of this kind. He encouraged Alec to find ways of behaving that could satisfy Alec's own needs while also respecting the needs of others.

On the few occasions when the younger brother was present, Richard was able to confirm much of what had already been said and to act as a valuable "go-between." Of all the boys in the family, young Richard was probably the closest to his parents. At the same time he had a warm relationship with Alec.

With the pastor's encouragement, the family sought for ways to help Alec feel more like a part of the family. Alec's father made a greater effort to communicate with his son. The mother sought to reduce her workload, and to be home at crucial times. Pastor Carrington invited a friendly young man from the church youth group to relate with Alec. This young man was almost fanatically devoted to motorbikes and cars, so he and Alec had an important interest in common. He befriended Alec and helped him get to know other members of the youth group who had similar interests. He also made a point of getting to know a few of Alec's friends in the gang.

In the individual counseling sessions, David used fantasy exercises. He invited Alec to close his eyes, relax, and imagine himself as the person he would like to be five years down the road. Alec was encouraged to *become* that person in his fantasy and to experience what it felt like. Alec saw himself as an independent and free twenty-year-old, one who was able to please himself and had many friends. Alec also expressed some interest in eventually becoming an automobile mechanic. Through warm positive responses, the pastor sought to encourage in Alec the development of long-term goals.

Occasionally he also sought to expand Alec's thinking about positive values by discussing with him various moral issues that surfaced in newspaper articles and features. Alec gradually gained confidence in verbalizing some of his own ideas about such issues.

Although Alec seemed to be making progress, he eventually left both home and job for several weeks. He again became involved with the gang in car stealing. For the time being this brought an end to regular counseling. The last message Pastor Carrington received from the Browns, however, reported that Alec had just returned home. He was starting a new job at a service station, and the parents now felt able to cope with the problem. The young man and several other friends from the youth group were still maintaining contact with Alec.

In his work with Alec, Pastor Carrington was attempting to apply certain counseling principles derived from two sources —reality therapy and family-oriented therapy. David sought to bring these two sets of principles together and to build them into a Christian framework.

Reality Therapy

Hobart Mowrer, a supporter of reality therapy, criticized Freud for not taking guilt seriously, for treating all guilt as neurotic. The basic problem in neurosis, Mowrer argued, is the real guilt that arises in consequence of wrong actions. "Human beings get into emotional binds," he says, "not because their standards are too high, but because their performance has been, and is, too low."* People tend to deny or disown messages from their own consciences. They do not face up to the wrongs they have done.

Mowrer's critique represented an important swing of the pendulum, but as so often happens the pendulum swung too far. Some of his insights are valuable, namely that real guilt can be a major factor in emotional distress and that the messages of a good and sensitive conscience are not to be disowned. To claim, however, that real guilt is the root cause of all neurosis, as Mowrer seems to be saying, is to claim far too much. We saw in the previous chapter that the inappropriate guilt of a punitive conscience can be a major source of emotional difficulty.

As Edward Stein points out in a helpful critique of Mowrer's theory, there is usually an interweaving of, and an interacting between, real guilt and neurotic guilt.† Mowrer's theory does not do justice to the complexities of human situations involving guilt. Many different types of conscience problems exist, and different therapeutic approaches are needed for each type.

Psychiatrist William Glasser, who developed reality therapy, has views similar to those of Mowrer.* Glasser's approach is helpful in counseling with people like Alec, people whose consciences seem weak or underdeveloped. One of the strengths of reality therapy is that it treats the problems of values and morality seriously. The counselor first establishes a warm relationship with the counselees and then begins to insist that these persons face the reality of their behavior and accept responsibility for it. Confrontation is an important dimension of such therapy. Personal needs, such as the need for love and for a sense of worth, are recognized. But persons are taught to fulfill these needs in responsible ways, that is in ways that do not prevent others from fulfilling their needs as well. The emphasis is on achieving constructive behavior rather than on developing enhanced insight. Whereas Freud sought to move from changed attitudes to changed behavior, Glasser emphasizes the reverse process, believing that changed behavior leads to changed attitudes.

The importance of first establishing a good relationship cannot be overemphasized. And that relationship needs to be genuine, not just a device for cushioning a later confrontation! To put it theologically, judgment comes appropriately within a context of grace and love. David Carrington opened the way for Alec Brown to be confronted by his parents, and for the parents to be confronted by Alec, but first the pastor concentrated on relationship building. Afterwards he also helped Alec and his parents to reflect on some of the issues raised in these confrontations. Since the parents were confessing Christians, David encouraged them to view these issues in the light of the gospel.

There is an important place for moral confrontation in helping relationships develop and grow. In recent years a number of writers have argued for a more responsible concern about moral issues within the practice of pastoral care and counseling.† John Hoffman makes a persuasive appeal for a recognition that true healing (even psychological healing) must involve a confrontation with the moral realities of life."* In care and counseling we need to avoid the coercive moralism often associated with negative conscience, and at the same time maintain a sense of ethical responsibility by consistently seeking to foster constructive consciences.

A Family-Oriented Approach

The methods of reality therapy often need to be supplemented by other approaches, such as those derived from the principles of family therapy. As we have seen, the consciences of the various members of a family are dynamically interrelated. The conscience of one is affected by changes and trends in the conscience of the others. Alec's underdeveloped conscience, for example, was in part a reaction against the conscientious, anxious, work-oriented consciences of his parents. Whenever Alec's conscience seemed to grow more complacent than before, his parents' consciences became even more anxious.

In the interactions of conscience between parents and children, a parent can sometimes unconsciously encourage a child to act out impulses and behavior patterns that for the parent were forbidden. This is more and more likely to happen as society becomes increasingly permissive. A mother who from early childhood has internalized strict standards about sexual behavior may be subtly encouraging her daughter to become involved in premature sexual relationships. A father may unconsciously encourage an aggressiveness in his son that he cannot tolerate in himself. What appears to be the strict conscience of the parent is then in dynamic interaction with the apparently weak conscience of the offspring, a conscience that seemingly has some significant gaps or "blind spots." This may well have been true in the relationship between Mr. Brown and Alec.

Conscience gaps of this kind are sometimes called "superego lacunae."† The superego lacunae of the child may duplicate similar unconscious defects in the consciences of the parents, which in turn come from defects in the consciences of *their* parents. Thus do the hidden sins of the parents eventually appear in the children!

A family-oriented approach, in which the pastor or counselor works mainly with the total family, and with subsystems within that family, can be helpful in dealing constructively with such interacting consciences. The degree to which you as a pastor or carer can work in this fashion with a total family will depend upon your previous training and background in family pastoral care.* All pastors, however, need to take as much account as possible of family interactions and structures. It is usually helpful if two pastors or carers of the opposite sex work together with a particular family, provided this is acceptable to the family in counseling. The pastors are likely to improve their counseling skills as they learn from each other, and additional resources are thereby provided for the family.

Strengthening Personal Values

People with weak or underdeveloped consciences do not often take the initiative in seeking help; their motivation for seeking help with a particular problem is likely to be low. More often a spouse, parent, relative, or teacher who is disturbed by their questionable behavior is the first to consult the pastor or counselor. The pastor may eventually need to send a special invitation to the person in question, suggesting a visit and talk. If the invitation is accepted, the counselor needs to work hard at building a warm relationship in which trust and respect can develop.

When Carol Martin came to share her distress with Pastor Keith Mitchell, she reported that her husband Bill was having an affair with his secretary. Carol said that Bill did not seem to care about her. Initially the pastor had three counseling sessions with Carol. Only then did he write a friendly, carefully worded letter to her husband, inviting Bill to come on his own and talk. Keith expressed a desire to meet Bill and hear his views on the situation and feelings about it. Keith said that this would help him, as a pastoral counselor, to better understand the total situation. Keith added that he would fully respect Bill's decision if he felt unable to come, though he would be disappointed not to meet Bill. Fortunately, after considerable hesitation, Bill responded positively to Keith's invitation. The pastor then had the difficult task of building a warm and friendly relationship. He hoped to move gradually toward a joint interview with both Carol and Bill.

Pastor Mitchell found that behind Bill's seeming lack of conscience were some genuine values. He helped Bill verbalize these values. Bill, for instance, had strong convictions about marriage, about the kind of relationship that should exist between a husband and wife. He said that his relationship with Carol had disappointed him. Keith helped Bill to identify some of the positive values embodied in his convictions and to reflect further on them. At this stage Keith did not express either agreement or disagreement with Bill's values; he simply concentrated on trying to understand them. In this way the pastor was able to help Bill clarify and develop his thinking about some of his values—a necessary step in the strengthening of positive conscience.

It was not until their third counseling session, after a friendly relationship had been established, that Keith invited Bill to consider the effect of his behavior on Carol. Moral confrontation now became an important dimension of the counseling process. Keith's manner and approach made it clear that he was willing not only to confront but also to be confronted. It also became clear to Bill that the pastor's counseling methods were not just the application of a professional technique, but an expression of a personal way of relating. Keith and Bill were eventually able to share their differing values and beliefs quite freely, without threatening the relationship. Genuine moral confrontation, within a relationship marked by mutual respect, facilitates the growth of positive conscience.

Some people express their values and goals more freely through drawings and paintings than through the use of words. They may respond warmly to an invitation to draw pictures of their family or pictures which express their feelings about their marriage, the future, death, or masculinity and femininity. It should be made clear that artistic technique is not what is being tested. In fact it is better if the picture is made without too much forethought or conscious effort. Such drawings or paintings can often trigger a significant verbal sharing of values within the counseling relationship.

Confrontation with one's own dreams can help to awaken a dormant conscience. Carl Jung tells of a businessman who was offered a business deal that would have involved him in fraud.* The man had no conscious feelings of guilt about accepting the offer, but in a dream it was clear that his hands and forearms were covered with dirt. Recalling that dream helped the man come to terms with the ethical issues involved. Dreams are not usually as clear as this in their meaning. However the retelling of a dream in a counseling context, with discussion of its possible significance, is often helpful for conscience development.

The Cognitive Dimensions of Conscience

Pastors and other leaders in a church community have the task of fostering concerned and positive action on important moral issues. One of the best ways to do this is through the development of small groups in which there is both personal caring and a responsible concern about social and political questions. Significant steps in this direction can be made already with children and adolescents. Small-group discussion of moral dilemma stories, of the type used by Jean Piaget and Lawrence Kohlberg in their research, is one way of stimulating this development.†

Piaget and Kohlberg sought to identify the stages of moral thinking through which people pass as they grow towards moral maturity. Piaget concluded from his research that young children initially regard moral rules as sacred and unchangeable. By the time of early adolescence the rules are gradually internalized and autonomous moral thinking develops. Eventually rules are no longer regarded as unalterable and there is a growing concern about issues of justice.

Kohlberg indentified six stages of moral development. In stage 1, moral thinking is dominated by the desire to avoid punishment. In stage 2, right is whatever satisfies one's own needs and possibly the needs of others. In stage 3, good behavior is what gains the approval of others. Stage 4 is the "law and order" stage: good behavior consists in obeying rules and respecting authority. For stage 5, the "social contract" stage, right is determined by standards that have been agreed upon by the whole society. In stage 6, good behavior is defined by decisions of conscience that are in accord with self-chosen moral principles of justice and love; of basic importance at this stage is respect for the dignity of all human beings.

In his research Kohlberg presented to his subjects a series of moral dilemma stories. He asked them to suggest what the people in the stories should do to deal with the dilemma. The subjects were told to give reasons for their recommendations. Kohlberg was interested in the reasons for the judgments rather than in the moral judgments themselves. The type of reason a person gave was considered an indication of that person's stage of moral maturity.

Moral dilemma stories are useful for both counseling and educational purposes. Within a group, those who are a stage ahead in moral development can often stimulate and challenge others, though if they are too far ahead others may not see the sense or relevance of what they are saying. In a sensitive way leaders of such groups raise questions about the members' responses to moral dilemma stories. They seek to encourage trends toward more mature moral thinking.

The stories to be used should be graded and sequenced in such a way that they gradually focus on ever more sensitive issues. Leaders and counselors can write stories of their own that are likely to be suitable for their particular group members or counseling clients. Some stories may ask whether a particular action is right or wrong, or whether a person should do one thing or another. Other stories may ask whether one person's actions are better or worse than those of another. Responding to these questions involves comparing different sets of values and making decisions about how values are best expressed. Following Kohlberg, leaders and counselors should place the emphasis on the reasons for moral judgment rather than on the judgments themselves.

One of Kohlberg's stories tells of fourteen-year-old Joe who wanted to go to camp. Joe's father told him he could go if he saved the money himself. So Joe worked hard at selling papers and saved up the forty dollars needed for the camp, plus a little more. Just before camp time, the father changed his mind; he needed some money himself to go on a fishing trip with friends and told Joe to give him the forty dollars that he had saved. Should Joe refuse his father or not? Why?*

This is a good story to use with adolescent boys, because it involves a boy's relationship with a father who acted unjustly. Responses to the questions asked by the story will give a leader or counselor some clues as to the boys' stage of moral development. The response should indicate whether an adolescent boy is still at a "heteronomous" (punishment) stage of morality or on the threshold of an autonomous sense of justice. Other stories could be given later to challenge him to move on to the next stage of moral judgment. It is not difficult of course to construct similar stories that would relate to adolescent girls. Such stories can develop the cognitive dimensions of conscience by stimulating reflection and thoughtful decision making.

Social Action and Pastoral Care

The awakening of a positive conscience concerned about important social issues can help to prevent some of the problems associated with weak and inadequate consciences. It can help to satisfy what Viktor Frankl calls the "will to meaning," which for him is the most basic of human needs.† Such a conscience gives people a cause, a basis for commitment that can become an integrating force in their lives, preventing anxiety-provoking purposelessness.

The fostering of various forms of group life within the believing community, in which value issues are discussed in a dialogical manner in the light of the gospel, can help to bring about an awakening of conscience in many areas of life where there have been conscience blind spots in the past. There is need for groups of this kind to focus on a whole range of human problems—sexism, racism, ecology, human rights, peace and war, family life, health, drug and alcohol abuse, the aged, the disabled, the unemployed. Wherever possible, such group discussions should lead to constructive action in the community.

Fantasy exercises may sometimes be used in small groups or in counseling to raise important social issues. After relaxing and breathing deeply, with eyes closed, a person may be invited to imagine a conversation with a victim of robbery or assault, or a victim of hunger, poverty, desertion, or oppression. The person first talks with the imaginary victim, then *becomes* that victim, expressing feelings about the distressful situation. The exercise continues with repeated reversal of roles. After the exercise there should be an opportunity for debriefing. Exercises of this kind can help to develop greater sensitivity toward human need.

The development of a conscience that is concerned about some worthy cause in the community can be an appropriate way of completing a counseling program. The cause taken up may be related to the person's problem. A person who has worked through a major grief problem, for example, may be invited to befriend other grief sufferers, or perhaps lead a grief recovery group. Many counseling clients respond to such invitations with enthusiasm; having been through the experience themselves, they can often become effective helpers. Ideally, helping others with personal problems is combined with a concern to do something about the social factors that tend to cause such problems.

As Alcoholics Anonymous has discovered, when people who have battled with problems are caught up in a meaningful mission to help others, they usually see their problems in a different perspective. These problems can become a means of service, helping to build bridges to others who are isolated or alienated. For members of the Christian community, their mission will be a part of the mission of the church, which is to cooperate with God's saving work in the world. All such healing work may be seen as a part of the creative transformation that Christ is continually effecting in human life.

4. The Confused Conscience

In the early years of my ministry, when destitute alcoholics came to the door of our manse and asked for money, I often experienced inner discomfort and conflict. In childhood I had been taught by church and home that it is good to give to the needy. So a deep dimension of conscience was urging me to give. Later experience and reflection, however, had taught me that it is usually not helpful to give money to a person suffering from alcoholism. The money almost always is spent on alcohol. By supporting the person's dependence on alcohol, I contribute to its continuation.

There was a time when I felt guilty whatever I did in this situation. If I refused to give money, I felt that I was rejecting the needy person in an un-Christian way. If I gave money, reason told me I was doing more harm than good. Sometimes I experienced additional guilt because I thought I should be doing more to help eradicate the social conditions which give rise to such problems. Nowadays my conscience is not quite so confused, partly because in place of money I offer such things as a meal, a place to sleep, and information about resources for help. Such alternative assistance is by no means a perfect solution. The things I offer are quite often refused, sometimes with anger, and I am still uneasy after my visitor has departed.

Reflection on experiences of this kind suggests that some value confusions and conflicts are the result of the diverse pressures coming upon us from different levels of conscience. Some "oughts" and "shoulds" come from the superego level, some from the level of moral reasoning, and some from social influences through peer groups. An adolescent, for example, may experience conflict between the internalized values derived from parents and teachers, the values absorbed through participation in the church community, the values arrived at by way of rational deliberation, and the values adopted from friends and peer groups. These diverse sets of values are not likely to be totally at odds with one another, but there will surely be important differences of emphasis between them. This kind of value confusion is accentuated in situations of social unrest and of family instability such as mark much of society today.

Contemporary Value Confusion

Abraham Maslow, who was a major spokesman for humanistic psychology, said that we are living today "in an interregnum between old value systems that have not worked and new ones not yet born."* Many people reject or ignore traditional systems of values, but find it difficult to replace them. We are surrounded by divergent and frequently changing value systems that compete for our allegiance. Sometimes these systems are wholly contradictory. Confusion or uncertainty about values is thus widespread, and this tends to increase interpersonal conflict and personal insecurity. Unfortunately the church shares in this value confusion and even contributes to it. Within the church as well as within the wider community there are major conflicts about moral issues.

The present situation of moral ambiguity and confusion profoundly affects people's consciences. The issues here are too complex for a simple description and interpretation, but I will refer to one or two major social trends. Reference has already been made to the increasing permissiveness and pluralism of Western society and to the growing questioning of authority. On most ethical issues there is no longer one "superego" kind of morality. Rather there is a wide range of moral attitudes and actions from which people can choose. This is why reason must play an increasingly important role in value judgments. While this pluralism makes for greater freedom in personal decision making, people who lack confidence in their capacity for sound moral judgment often experience commensurately great uncertainty and anxiety.

According to Allen Wheelis, it is not just that the superego has become weaker; there has also been a shrinking of the realm over which it exercises authority.* On a vast range of matters relating to sexual behavior, for example, many people feel free to follow their own viewpoints rather than conform to traditional standards or to the pronouncements of institutions like the church.

Peer groups exercise a powerful influence in today's society. Most people belong to a variety of vocational, recreational, educational, or religious groups. These groups develop their own norms and values. Peer-group members are generally expected to conform to the values of their group, even those with which they may not personally agree. The values of the various groups to which an individual belongs may differ quite widely from each other and from the standards learned in the family. Value confusion and conflict are almost inevitable.

The individual is often caught in a dilemma. On the one hand, commitment to clearly defined and worthwhile values helps to build a durable sense of identity, which is a basic human need. On the other hand, such a commitment can complicate peer relationships. This is a serious problem particularly for adolescents, who are trying to sort out basic identity and value problems and who at the same time depend so heavily on peer-group support.

Values and Counseling

Value confusion or conflict is likely to be a major factor in many of the problems brought by people seeking pastoral care and counseling. An important goal for the church's teaching and pastoral ministry is to help people work through their confusion about values and develop more coherent, realistic, and responsible values that accord with the values expressed in Christ's life and teaching. This is no easy task, especially since pastors, counselors, and leaders are struggling themselves to find values that are both genuinely Christian and authentically their own. We pastoral counselors cannot attempt to give authoritative answers to all the value problems brought to us. What we can do—and this is more helpful—is to provide a caring and supportive environment in which values may be clarified and strengthened and, when necessary, revised so as to reflect more faithfully the values of Christ.

Jill Kennedy, the eighteen-year-old college student mentioned in chapter 1, remained after the Friday night meeting of the church youth group to talk with one of the youth leaders, Sarah White. Jill was confident that Sarah could help her. She knew that Sarah was a trained counselor and a fairly recent college graduate. When Jill complained that she was "mixed up" and needed "sorting out," Sarah suggested that they sit down and talk.

Jill said she was beginning to feel as if she did not really belong in the group: "In the past I really enjoyed being part of the group, but I guess I'm changing." Jill realized that she was being influenced by some fairly radical college friends who had little or no association with the church—she liked their concern for oppressed and disadvantaged people. These college friends were also teaching her to question some of her Christian beliefs and values, especially those relating to morality. Jill's Christian values had been important to her since early high school days. Now she was feeling threatened by mounting questions and doubts. Jill told Sarah that while she had recently become more radical in her thinking, most members of the church youth group seemed to have become more conservative in their religious and political views. Though group members were still outwardly friendly toward her, Jill felt that inwardly they disapproved of her. "I feel both guilty and angry," she said, "guilty for changing my views and angry with the group because they are not more flexible and open in their outlook." Jill assured Sarah that faith in God was still very important to her and that she had been praying for guidance.

Other issues were also aggravating the situation. Jill had recently broken a twelve-month relationship with her boyfriend, a member of the church youth group, mainly because she felt they were not really suited to each other. She was also finding her studies very demanding and at times tedious; she wondered whether she should drop out of college. She had received an invitation to live for a year or more on an uncle's farm several hundred miles away. This appealed to her very much. Another attractive possibility was to take a course in catering; Jill said she had been to a number of church camps and conferences as a member of the catering staff and loved the work.

As she shared the feeling of being almost torn apart, pulled in many different directions at once, Jill wept freely. Sarah White not only listened but responded with warmth and offered support. She inquired whether any of the people close to Jill were influencing her feelings and decision making. Jill said that her parents had not shown much understanding of her situation. Her mother, a high-school teacher involved in the church, wanted Jill to remain in the church and to complete her college courses; Jill said that her mother tended to dominate her and was ambitious for her future. Her father, a successful businessman, was only loosely linked with the church, but he had strict views about sexual morality. He favored Jill's leaving college to escape the influence of the radical students. However he did not press his views. Whenever there was conflict in the home he tended to withdraw.

As the hour was late, Sarah invited Jill to come to her home in a few days to continue their conversation. There Sarah helped Jill to identify in more specific terms some of the main differences between the viewpoints of her college friends and those of the church youth group. She encouraged Jill to look at a few of the main issues as objectively as she could, separating the issues themselves from the people with whom they had become associated. She suggested that Jill discuss some of the theological and value issues with their pastor, Keith Mitchell, for whom Jill had considerable respect. Then Sarah invited Jill to express her feelings about the friends themselves. Sarah even helped Jill become quite specific in describing the difference in her feelings toward her college friends and toward the church group.

Sarah helped Jill make a clear separation between her short-term and long-term goals. To clarify the long-term goals, Sarah invited Jill to share in a fantasy exercise, picturing herself as the person she would like to be in ten years. Jill saw herself as eventually a wife and mother, as a professional person with leadership responsibilities, and—though she was less sure about this—as an active leader in the church. In subsequent discussion, Jill began to feel that her uncle's farm and the catering course offered primarily an escape from her painful conflicts, the confused relationship with her boyfriend, and the struggle for independence from her parents, especially her mother. She realized that it was more important for her to face her conflicts and struggles and to work them through. She felt that her recent radical tendencies and her desire to drop out of college were, in part, an expression of her need to show that she could be independent of her mother; together Jill and Sarah explored other ways of expressing this healthy need for independence. On the other hand, the discussions also led Jill to become in some respects even more deeply committed to certain of her radical views.

Having established good rapport and made some progress together, Sarah now gained Jill's agreement for a joint meeting involving her parents as well. Sarah encouraged Jill to share with her parents directly her feelings of confusion and conflict. Sarah wanted to help Jill's parents become less rigid and more understanding than they had been in the past. She hoped that a constructive change in the parents' consciences would give Jill the freedom to develop a conscience that was not only caring and responsible but also genuinely her own. Sarah found conversation with the parents difficult. Jill's mother was tense; the father quiet. However, Mr. and Mrs. Kennedy did seem to gain some understanding of Jill's conflicts. Encouraged by Sarah, the parents were also able to convey to Jill some of their own needs for support.

Sarah and Jill met together on three more occasions. At the end of the second of these three conversations Sarah suggested to Jill that they make a list of about fifteen activities in which Jill had some interest, such as music, cooking, dancing, worship, study, caring for children. That done, she asked Jill to think at home about the importance of these activities, to rank them in order of their value to her, and to bring the results to the next session. Jill was free to add more activities to the list if she wished.

Jill reported at their next visit that she had not found this an easy task, but it had helped her in sorting out her values. Worship and study, it seemed, ranked high on her list, so she felt confirmed in her college program and in her place in the church community. She felt that her decision to continue her studies was now her own decision rather than merely an acquiescence to her mother's wishes. She planned to review her college situation again after that year in light of her final grades. Jill also felt more confident now in expressing her own views, both among her college friends and among members of the church youth group. With enhanced understanding of how her own values had developed, she was learning to be more tolerant of views that differed from her own. She had contacted her boyfriend again and, although nothing had been decided about the future, she thought they would probably be seeing each other regularly. Sarah then focused Jill's attention on long-term goals, helping her to experience the call to Christian adulthood. She encouraged Jill to talk with her again if further crises occurred. She also expressed confidence in Jill's ability to cope with her present situation.

Making Value Choices

To work constructively with confused consciences, a pastor needs some understanding of the process involved in making value choices. When something is of special value to us, we choose it in preference to other things. We are likely to cherish what we have chosen, and that choice is likely to affect our subsequent actions.

I value books, especially books on psychology and religion, so when I go to the large shopping center in our community I choose to visit the bookstore, and there I choose to browse in a certain section of the store. I usually drive home from the shopping center with a new book on the seat beside me. If it has been a good buy, I cherish the book and show it to my wife.

However, I may also have some guilty feelings about having spent the money on a book rather than on food or clothing or other basics needed in the home.

Choosing, cherishing, acting, and feeling are all involved in the valuing process. This also applies to behavior in which moral issues are obviously at stake. Any positive value choices also imply value negations—other possible choices were *not* pursued. There may be guilt feelings with respect to the values that were ignored or rejected. Sometimes our value choices and the actions consequent upon them are deliberate; there is conscious decision making. At other times we are largely unaware that our decisions and actions are in fact expressive of the values we hold.

The Gospel accounts of the temptations of Jesus provide one kind of model for making value choices.* At the outset of his ministry, Jesus was confronted with various possible patterns of ministry, each embodying different values and principles. These patterns of ministry raised some of the basic value issues with which Jesus struggled before committing himself to the public ministry in Galilee. There were three possibilities: (1) to use his powers to meet his own needs; (2) to become a great king in a worldly sense, thereby bringing prosperity and happiness to many; or (3) to put God to the test in a spectacular demonstration of power, thereby showing the great power of faith. Each of these possibilities was faced, considered, and firmly rejected. The choices were not forced by circumstances or by pressure from others; they were deliberately made. Jesus' relationship with God and reliance on the teachings of Scripture guided him in his rejection of each temptation and in his strong commitment to the way of caring and suffering love.

Unfortunately, most of us rarely make value decisions in this deliberate, intentional, prayerful way. More often we choose and act out of habit, or in response to the pressure of circumstances, or as a means of social adjustment. Rarely do we make positive, intentional value choices with the help of God and in the light of his word. We can all use help in clarifying our values.

Clarifying Values

Carl Rogers makes a useful distinction between "operative" values and "conceived" values.* The former term refers to value choices embodied in a person's behavior, choices that may have been made with little or no conscious thought; my usual busy behavior, for example, may indicate that I value busyness, though I have never made a conscious decision about busyness as a value for my life. A conceived value, on the other hand, expresses a conscious choice; it is the result of decision making, with anticipation of the results of the decision. Both types of values are important and no sharp line of separation should be drawn between them. To distinguish between them, however, can be helpful for an understanding of the process of values clarification.

Operative and Conceived Values

In values clarification, past or habitual value choices are reflected on, reassessed, and where necessary revised. Values clarification fosters conscious awareness of one's operative values, making it possible for those values to be reassessed. This reassessment should lead to choices that are more deliberately made and express conceived values that are genuinely cherished.

There are various value indicators that people can use to measure the motivating strength of their operative values. These value indicators are provided by the answers to such questions as the following: "How do you spend your time?" "How do you spend your money?" "What things do you worry about most?" "What makes you guilty or ashamed?" The answers to such questions can provide a list of values that are important motivators of a person's behavior. People then rank the listed values in their order of importance.

Other types of questions relate to what one might do in a crisis: "If you discovered that your house was on fire, what would you try to save?" "If you knew that you had only a few weeks to live, what would you most want to do in those few weeks?" "If you could choose not to be yourself, what person would you most like to be?" Such questions can help put people in touch with things they value highly and with qualities they greatly admire—to which they may previously have given little conscious attention.

Values clarification can be used in individual, family, and group counseling. Sarah White used some of the methods of values clarification to help Jill Kennedy become aware of the values that were most important to her. Pastoral counselors can help people to perceive clearly and to examine and assess their operative values. Issues can be raised and discussed relating to those values that may not have been previously considered. Where values are in conflict with each other, a counselor can provide a context in which those conflicts are faced, discussed, and possibly resolved. If some of a person's values have become destructive and hurtful to others, as in the case of highly manipulative behavior, ethical confrontation is likely to be involved in the counseling process, though the timing of such confrontation needs to be carefully considered. A relationship characterized by trust, warmth, and mutual respect needs to be established first. Further counseling can then bring these destructive values into the open, revealing what they are doing to people and how they conflict with other values the person holds.

Adolescents may be helped to look more closely at the secondhand values that are operative in their lives, whether derived from parents or from peer groups. This can nurture the development of moral autonomy. Parents of young children experiencing many conflicting demands upon their time often appreciate help in assessing priorities in their use of time and money. Some grief work may need to be done as the satisfactions associated with less important values are set aside. People in their middle years can gain a great deal if they are helped to become more aware of the destructive values that over the years have become increasingly powerful in their lives. This can be quite a shock at first. We can become so caught up in achieving, and in tasks associated with our work, that we are not even aware of how the values expressed by our daily patterns and priorities are in conflict with other values we highly prize.

Clergy persons in a values clarification exercise were quite shocked to discover the discrepancy between their conceived values and the operative values expressed by their use of time. Most said they regarded the family, personal relationships, relaxation, reading, and meditation as highly important in Christian living and in ministry, but these activities did not figure prominently in their daily programs. The crises of illness, hospitalization, and grief can bring a similar shocked but valuable awareness of the gap between conceived and operative values.

Fostering Values Awareness

Behind a counselee's problems, difficulties, and conflicts may be largely unrecognized personal values. Even people who seem to scorn worthwhile values often have positive ideals that are almost concealed by hostility and aggressiveness. A counselor's responses can help these hidden and perhaps confused values to become more explicit, so that they are available for clarification and revision. Counselors need to be alert and sensitive to respond to these hidden or half-hidden values. These pastoral responses are best phrased in a tentative way. Counselors can inquire as to whether they have correctly understood the deeper level of meaning being expressed. If a counselor is able to "pick up" these latent values, the counseling may then be able to move to a more constructive phase. One of the tasks of the counselor is to help a person or family become aware of the various levels at which conscience is operating and of the values being expressed in behavior at each of these levels. This helping process should assist in bringing clarity out of confusion and in developing values that are a genuine expression of the self.

Dreams

Confrontation with one's dreams can assist values clarification. According to the Gestalt view, all parts of a dream, both the human and the nonhuman parts, are a projection of some aspect of one's self.* If this is true, we can expect the various persons and objects in our dreams to express some of our values. If a person in counseling retells a dream in the first person and the present tense, as though the events of the dream are happening now, that person's values often emerge very clearly.

In an important dream of my own, I once dreamed that I was carefully cutting out a design from paper (my daughter had been doing some cutting out during the day) and I was very concerned about the contrast between the pleasing design I had cut out and the untidy mess of leftover paper scraps. As I reflected on the dream, it seemed to be saying to me that I spend a great deal of my time carving out a career and fulfilling various professional roles, but that I pay little attention to what is leftover, "the scraps" that make up the rest of my life. That dream caused me to think deeply about some of my priorities.

Peak Experiences

Another helpful procedure in values clarification is to invite the sharing of what Abraham Maslow called "peak experiences."† Peak experiences are moments of high inspiration, or revelation, or ecstasy, in which there is a feeling of oneness with God, with fellow human beings, and with the universe. These experiences are usually followed by deep feelings of serenity. The sharing of peak experiences, in either individual or group counseling, will almost inevitably convey values that are of importance to the person concerned.

One woman told me of a time when she felt an invisible hand guiding her through city streets, leading to a high moment of inspiration in a chapel where she believed God spoke to her. The chapel experience led to her gaining a new job as secretary of a church organization. Through this job she was able to perform a special service for God and the church. Though there were some unusual elements in the reported experiences, I was able to share with her a conviction that God had been working throughout her life in significant ways. Both the events she described and her interpretations of them pointed to life values that were of great importance to her. We were able to make use of these values in sorting out some of her problems.

Family Values

Values clarification can also be effectively used in family counseling. When working with a total family, it is often helpful to ask each family member to make a list of current family rules. These could include rules in a variety of areas: "Everybody keeps their own bedroom clean and tidy," "Everybody takes turns in setting the table and washing the dishes," "Everybody helps in the garden for at least half an hour on Saturday," "All the children are given adequate pocket money once a month." The family could then identify the values embodied in such rules and discuss whether these values are important for good family life. Following the discussion, the family may agree that some rules should be modified or dropped, and that others should be added. This helps to involve the whole family in clarifying values and in determining which values matter most. It also helps family members to become aware of conflicting values. At times they will have to agree to differ, or to accept some compromises, but at least each family member will be aware of the viewpoints of the others.

Christian Values in Counseling

From a Christian perspective it may be argued that values clarification in pastoral care and counseling has a serious limitation: it is restricted to matters of clarification and does not necessarily involve the development of better values. Has anything been gained if a person only clarifies but does not change values that are inadequate, unworthy, or destructive? Values clarification, as presented here however, is only part of the total process of value formation and reformulation in counseling. It represents only an interim goal rather than a final goal. Frequently it contributes significantly to the revision of values. Clarification of existing values can cause a person or family to decide that more adequate values are needed, and the forming of those more adequate values is an important part of the process of developing a creative, positive conscience.

A pastoral counselor will often want to raise with people value questions that they may not yet have considered. This should be done in a sensitive, concerned, and nonauthoritarian way. Again, at appropriate times, counselors will want to share their own values, not in an authoritarian way but as friend to friend discussing possible approaches to the problems under consideration. Pastors who share personal values in this way will always want to invite feedback and response.

Pastors working with members of their own Christian community may also wish to invoke the ministry of Jesus: "Let's look at our values, both yours and mine, in the light of the life, teachings, death, and resurrection of Jesus Christ." Such a suggestion presupposes that the biblical records, especially the accounts of Jesus' ministry and teachings, provide valid and helpful criteria for the assessment and revision of values. For people not burdened with neurotic guilt, a time of quiet meditation may be suggested in which some of their actions, past or contemplated, are viewed as though taking place in the presence of Christ. Such meditation sometimes means a powerful confrontation with the gospel. If guilt feelings are thereby aroused, they need to be verbalized and discussed. The message of God's forgiveness for those who trust him needs to be affirmed.

Counselors who participate in such an experience receive ministry as well as give ministry. All human values including clergy values appear limited and inadequate when viewed in the light of God's love in Jesus Christ. Such a meditative experience may be followed by a period of rich sharing, in which the prior experience of confrontation with the gospel is honestly faced, and values are discussed and revised. Reference may also be made to opportunities available at other times and places—in teaching, preaching, and reading as well as counseling—where Christian values are presented in a more systematic and comprehensive way.

5. The Righteous Conscience

At a pastoral care seminar Peter Scott, a recent seminary graduate, recalled one of the most difficult pastoral situations of his early ministry. Brian, a young man of seventeen, regularly assisted with the counting of the Sunday offerings in Peter's first congregation. Young Brian was the only child of a married couple who had been closely associated with the church for many years. After suspicion had been aroused that money might be disappearing from the collection plate, Brian was observed actually taking some of the offering. Peter and a few of the church elders tactfully confronted him. Brian simply shrugged his shoulders but then went home and told his mother about the incident. She was outraged! She could not believe that their only son could have done such a thing—after all, he had been reared in a good home and within the fellowship of the church. Feeling that the family had been utterly disgraced and insulted, she refused to return to the church, angrily rejecting all invitations from Peter and the elders. Her husband, a quiet and ineffective person, acquiesced in her decision.

Soon after this incident Brian left home and joined the army. In a sense the crisis had helped him to find the autonomy he needed. Both Brian and his parents, however, experienced a great deal of pain, and the bitterness was intense. At no stage did the family sit down and discuss the crisis together. The parents also remained alienated from the church.

In the discussion that followed Peter's presentation of the case, a member of the pastoral care seminar suggested that what kept the parents from helping Brian during the crisis was their need to defend and maintain a "righteous" conscience.

Seminar members generally agreed that such a conscience can indeed hinder the honest facing of a disturbing reality and can prevent effective caring.

Conscience and Oppression

"All my married life I've been desperately unhappy and lonely, though my husband is such a good man. Everyone looks up to him. But he makes me feel so inadequate." Kathy Newman, a woman in her forties, looked pale, tense, and tired as she poured out her feelings to her pastor, Doreen Jamison.

"We have four children and there's so much to do. Yet George never helps with meals or housework! He can't cook an egg! He quotes Scripture at me to show me that work of the home is a wife's responsibility. He has such fixed ideas about a woman's role. He tried to stop me from taking driving lessons. Even now he doesn't want me driving the car. He was angry about my getting a part-time job, even though it's only two days a week. But I have to have some interests outside the home if I'm to survive!" Kathy began to weep freely as she shared her distress.

"I don't want to sound ungrateful," she added, after a pause. "I know he means well. In his own way, George does love me. He's always been faithful to me. But he can become so jealous if I even look at another man. And he says that a husband *should* be jealous, because the Bible speaks of the Lord as a jealous God. When George leads our family devotions, his favorite passage is that one from Proverbs about the virtuous woman.* And when he reads it, I know he's really telling me what I should be like—that I'm not a satisfactory wife the way I am."

Pastor Jamison had often heard this kind of story. For some years she had specialized in working with married couples to help them find greater freedom and fulfillment in their relationships. Again and again she had encountered men with "righteous" and sexist consciences oppressing the consciences of their wives. At the same time, the wives were seeking to heed the call of conscience to an enhanced freedom and to a more varied and satisfying use of their gifts. Doreen had tried to help both wives and husbands find release from the stereo-typed behavior patterns and expectations which had imprisoned them. This usually involved breaking the power of a "righteous" conscience.

The Self-Righteous Conscience

In the sense in which I am using the term, a "righteous" conscience is essentially self-righteous. Persons with a dominantly righteous conscience generally live respectable lives, complying with the standards of their group and obeying an acceptable legal code. Their goodness, however, tends to be confined within the limits set by their own group, class, sex, culture, or religious denomination. Usually these persons are not even aware of their own rigidity and limitations, though they often have hidden fears about failure. They tend to see evil in people different from themselves.

Two different, though overlapping, types of righteous conscience can be distinguished. In the first of these, the conforming tendency dominates. People with a conforming conscience have a deep need to measure up to the current standards and expectations of their own group. They experience a sense of shame if they depart from the values of that group. Erik Erikson talks about the limitations and dangers of what he calls a "tribal" conscience.* Such a conscience shows a concern for "tribal" standards and for people belonging to the in-group or "tribe" but is intolerant and rejecting toward people outside that group and toward their values.

In the second type of righteous conscience, the legalistic orientation dominates. People with a legalistic conscience adhere to whatever legal or moral code has supreme status and authority. There is again a tendency to look down on people who do not subscribe to the revered code. This is the kind of conscience that found expression in the prayer: "God, I thank thee that I am not like other men, extortioners, unjust, adulterers, or even like this tax gatherer. I fast twice a week, I give tithes of all that I get."†

These two types of righteous conscience often merge into one, for a legal code is usually associated with a particular group or culture. The concern to conform to a group and the concern to adhere to a code then become one and the same.

On the other hand, the two do not always coincide. A legalistic conscience can become firmly established in childhood. Then in later life it may resist the influences of every peer group and not conform to any group standards.

From the time the righteous conscience first makes its appearance in childhood, attitudes associated with it often become increasingly pervasive and powerful. Both consciously and unconsciously, we develop many strategies for protecting a righteous conscience. It becomes bound up with our emotional and spiritual security. Such a conscience can effectively conceal serious doubts about our worthiness and acceptability. As in the case of Kathy Newman's husband, we may use religious beliefs and practices to maintain and defend our righteous conscience, without recognizing the destructive effect it has on others. When our conscience is threatened, we are likely to strengthen our defenses and attack those who threaten us. Brian's mother apparently felt threatened in this way. She expressed intense anger at the accusation that her son had stolen part of the offering, and she isolated herself from the threatening community.

As I write, I am myself aware of the temptation to point an accusing finger at others, and to see righteous conscience only in those groups and movements to which I do not belong. When I succumb to this temptation, I am displaying one of the characteristics of the kind of conscience here described. I need to remind myself that people with righteous consciences are not necessarily more blameworthy than those with negative or weak consciences. Righteous conscience processes are probably involved in all of us to some degree. The complexity of human beings is such that guilty and righteous feelings can coexist and interact within the same conscience.

Humanizing the Conscience

The humanizing of one's conscience involves a broadening of sympathies, a deepening of concern for others, and a growth in flexibility and understanding of those who are different from one's self. All of us need to have our limited consciences broken open and humanized by the grace of the God of all creation, who is concerned for people of all groups, systems, classes, races, and consciences.

Therapeutic Confrontation

People from a restricted, sheltered background sometimes have a complacent, righteous conscience because they have had little opportunity or challenge to grow beyond their native situation. Regular involvement in a small sharing group can help a person move beyond the confines of a narrow morality. This process is enhanced by the presence in the group of people with different backgrounds and diverse experience, people who are warm and sensitive yet ready to confront when confrontation seems appropriate. Unfortunately persons with a dominantly self-righteous conscience tend to avoid such groups —as indeed they tend to avoid counseling—fearing their security may be threatened.

Scapegoating

A "righteous" member of a family sometimes enters into counseling as a consequence of bringing a "problem" member of the family to a counselor for help. In such a situation so-called scapegoat processes are usually operative. Some family members keep their own conscience clear by disowning or submerging antisocial tendencies within themselves. They then project these tendencies onto another member of the family who in turn acts out these forbidden family wishes. Such scapegoaters are usually unaware of what they are doing. If a particular family member has always been somewhat difficult, he or she can easily be made the family scapegoat. The family system is then maintained by channeling most hostile feelings toward the one offender. When a husband and wife are angry with each other, for example, one of the children often catches their hostility. Where this scapegoat process is in operation, the pastoral counselor has the difficult task of helping the "righteous" members face and accept their own responsibility for some of the family problem.

The Context of Acceptance

Therapeutic confrontation usually needs to occur if "righteous" consciences are to become more constructive and caring. When Jesus confronted the rich young ruler possessed of a righteous conscience, he did so lovingly.* Jesus challenged the young man's limited, conforming conscience by inviting him to do things that went beyond the bounds of duty and customary obligation. In this incident Jesus gives us a model of therapeutic confrontation. His approach helped the young ruler's conscience become less self-righteous and more sensitive than it had been before. According to the synoptic Gospels Jesus openly confronted the Pharisees and their self-righteous conformity to the law, but he was warmly accepting of an individual Pharisee like Nicodemus. When confrontation occurs within counseling, it needs to be within the context of warm acceptance, and it should be followed by discussion, including an honest expression of feelings by all the parties involved.

Therapeutic confrontation often comes from another member of the family or group, though this usually needs to be monitored and guided by a pastor or counselor. In a counseling session with Doreen Jamison and a male pastor colleague who agreed to be her cocounselor, Kathy Newman confronted her husband about his rigid standards and role expectations. Having been guided by Doreen, Kathy was able to confront her husband mainly through "I" messages about herself that expressed her own needs, rather than through accusing "you" messages calculated to put him down.†

Building a "Statue"

In one family counseling session in which I was involved, the family members were invited to physically position the whole family in a kind of "statue" arrangement. The purpose of the "statue" was to give visible and tangible expression to the way in which family members perceived their relationships with each other. The nineteen-year-old "problem son," eldest in a family of four children, responded first. He placed his mother and her two teen-age daughters together, so that they were standing upright in one group, representing a power bloc. He and his younger brother squatted down opposite them, looking cowed. One of the counselors asked, "How about your father?" As the young man hesitated the father, a widely respected air force officer, looked ill at ease. Though actively involved in the community he had given little or no leadership within the family. He seemed bent on keeping his own conscience "clear" by avoiding all family arguments. The young man finally went over to his father and asked him to lie full length on the floor between the two groups as though he were asleep. The father reluctantly complied, and the "problem" member went back to rejoin his younger brother. There was a powerful silence in the room for what seemed like several minutes. The father was clearly feeling the impact of the confrontation. The therapy team of psychologist, social worker, and pastor then began a discussion of the whole issue that eventually involved everyone present; they reported that the "statue" reflected one way in which they too saw relationships within the family. This powerful confrontation in a context of acceptance led the father to reexamine his conscience. Eventually he decided that he must give more positive leadership in the home.

Mediation

In the pastoral care seminar referred to at the beginning of this chapter most members felt that Pastor Peter Scott could have made a greater effort to meet with the whole family—Brian and his mother and father—in the hope of opening up more meaningful communication among them. Peter agreed that it might have been possible to find a person in the congregation who could have mediated between the church and the alienated family. By working sensitively through such a person, Peter might have been able to arrange a family counseling session with both the mediating person and himself present.

The immediate goal of such a session would be to work toward more effective communication within the family. The long-term goal would be to seek a humanizing of the mother's conscience and a strengthening of the father's conscience and to help Brian develop constructive personal values that were genuinely his own.

Interpreting Dreams

A humanizing confrontation can also come about through the use of a person's dreams. Dreams sometimes express the dark, hidden, or ignored side of a personality. Discussion and interpretation of dreams can often lead to modification and enlargement of conscience as people come to terms with those darker dimensions which they usually reject or avoid. One of Carl Jung's male patients, for example, regularly dreamed of a drunken and disheveled woman.* Jung interpreted this as an expression of the "female" dimension of the dreamer, the so-called anima. The dream thus expressed "the deplorable condition of the woman within." It balanced the man's conscious tendency to see himself as a perfect gentleman. Encounter with the dream helped the man to the enlargement and humanizing of his conscience. Viktor Frankl similarly tells of a woman who through confrontation with one of her dreams, as interpreted by Frankl, became aware that she was tormenting her daughter with exaggerated demands for moral "cleanliness," and that the mother was in danger of losing her daughter.† We may properly be uncertain about the validity of any particular dream interpretation. However a discussion of possible interpretations can help to confront, challenge, and change the everyday conscience.

Facing the Shadow

A basic theological issue involved in this process of humanizing the righteous conscience concerns the nature of human evil. The Bible confirms the fact that human evil can sometimes have a very "righteous" or pious appearance. Paul indicates that basic human sinfulness is involved when human beings worship themselves rather than God—when the creature, or that which the creature has made, takes the place of God (Rom. 1:25). The essence of sin, then, is pride or arrogance, an assumed greatness. Sin can infect everything we do; it has both personal and communal dimensions. It can even enter into and corrupt our religious observances and our "unselfish" service. These activities often become tainted by self-worship. Thus our deepest sins are spiritual in nature. We can be very clever in deceiving ourselves. We can enjoy a "good" conscience in the midst of our personal and social evil.

Jung's concept of "the shadow" can be helpful in expounding and developing this biblical view of evil.* The shadow, according to Jung, is that dark, "inferior" side of the personality which, as we have seen, sometimes makes itself known in dreams. It is an expression of feelings and tendencies that a person does not easily admit into conscious awareness. Jung does not directly identify the shadow with unmitigated evil. He does see it as embodying powerful forces of evil, as well as having potential for good. We humans tend to identify ourselves with light and consciousness, with what we willingly acknowledge as open and aboveboard. We tend to disown our shadow, thereby keeping our conscience clear. So within the personality there is a kind of split between light and darkness, good and evil. However, this human process of disowning the shadow does not destroy it. The shadow continues to exercise a powerful influence in our lives even though we are largely unaware of it. Our shadow often is projected onto other individuals or groups. We tend to project onto them the evil we cannot accept in ourselves. This projecting is actually the basic process in the scapegoating to which we earlier referred.

For wholeness, I need to recognize my shadow and learn to live with it; I need to integrate it with the conscious dimensions of my life. The assurance that God accepts my whole self, including my shadow, helps give me the courage to accept myself as I am. Such acceptance brings an enlargement of consciousness and a humanization of conscience. To the degree that I honestly face the dark and rejected side of my life, to that degree I am freed from the need to label and attack others—and from the need to hold on to a false image of my own goodness. By coming to terms with their own shadow, pastors are enabled better to assist others in the humanizing of their righteous conscience processes.

Goodness and the Child

The biblical concept of "the child" throws light on the nature of the goodness with which the gospel is concerned. It is very significant that in the synoptic Gospels it is "the child," rather than the "righteous" adult, who symbolizes entrance into the kingdom of God. Despite interference and objection by his disciples, Jesus received the infants who were brought to him. On the other hand the rich young man, who came to Jesus with all his achievements and accomplishments, both material and moral, "went away sorrowful."* Jesus used "the child" as a symbol of what needs to happen in that act of repentance which leads into the kingdom.† Unless we repent and become open, receptive, trusting, and playful like young children, we will not experience the liberation and joy of the kingdom.

The process of "becoming as a child" includes a growing awareness of the presence of the inner child. This new awareness can lead to a liberation of the child dimension in each of us so that it fulfills its proper role in adult life. Transactional Analysis as developed by Eric Berne, Muriel James, and others, has helped to bring a new recognition of the importance of this child dimension in adult living.‡ TA has shown how some expressions of "the child" can be destructive in adult life, as when the so-called Adapted Child is still trying to satisfy the internalized demands of one or both parents.

An active "Natural Child" is associated with spontaneity, genuineness, joy, and creativity; it can help to maintain these positive qualities in the life of an adult. If this healthy inner child has become submerged through the demands of adult living, a rediscovery of its life-giving qualities can be a profound, humanizing experience. I do not directly identify this kind of emotional experience with the process of "becoming as a child" before God. However, I believe the two processes overlap considerably: authentic Christian conversion often includes a rediscovery of spontaneity, genuineness, joy, and creativity.

Liberating the Inner Child

Fantasy experiences of various kinds can often be used effectively in counseling situations designed to initiate some liberation of the inner child. This liberation can result in greater spontaneity and flexibility in daily living and a humanizing of righteous conscience processes. If vitality is to be restored to adult life, says Fritz Perls, it is necessary "to recover the child's way of experiencing the world."* These fantasy exercises can be used with an individual or in a group setting. They should be followed by a thorough sharing of experiences and feelings by the people involved.

We may invite people to relax and imagine scenes from their early childhood, especially scenes likely to be associated with excitement and joy, such as a birthday party, celebration of Christmas, mealtime, or going on vacation. For some, these old experiences will be associated more with pain than with joy. Therefore it is important first to check out the nature of the associations for the people involved. The invitation is given to imagine the childhood scene, to imagine what the people present—and others about them—would have been saying, doing, and feeling, and then to reenter that scene in order to experience old feelings again.

Another procedure is for the counselor to act as a child and to invite the other person or persons to do the same. It is helpful if the basic principles of TA are well known. The counselor may begin: "I am five years old and have not yet been to school. You are whatever age you choose, but under eight."† All participants then seek to use the language and to express the feelings and attitudes regarded as appropriate to the ages chosen. The exercise can be good fun, and can help to arouse childlike feelings that may have been hidden for a long time.

A variation on the above procedures is to invite a person to imagine that he or she is with a child of the same sex, playing on a beach or in a meadow or park, as in the following exercise:

> Make yourself comfortable and close your eyes; relax your muscles by tensing and releasing them; breathe deeply and smoothly, allowing the tensions to flow out of you as you exhale; center your attention for a time on your breathing. . . . Now imagine yourself playing with a young child of the same sex as yourself on a beach (meadow, park); you are both enjoying yourselves; put yourself into the picture as the adult; what are you doing with the child? what are you saying? what are you feeling? what does the little child look like? what is he (she) doing? Get in touch with your feelings. . . . Now *become* the child; what are you doing and saying to the adult? what does it feel like? . . . Now become the adult again. Keep reversing the roles for a short time; open your eyes and debrief.

Fantasies of this kind can help to generate profoundly moving experiences, possibly bringing torrents of tears, as dimensions of the self long lost and buried burst forth into life again. There needs to be time after such an experience for extensive debriefing and follow-up counseling. I find that such exercises often help to liberate deeper sympathies and sensitivity, and a greater degree of caring. They result in a strengthening of the constructive positive conscience.

6. The Maturing Healthy Conscience

The development of a maturing healthy conscience is a major goal of pastoral care and counseling and of preventive education. The church's caring dare not become totally absorbed in the many problems clamoring for pastoral attention. Where pastoral care is oriented towards conscience it should be concerned mainly to foster the growth of a healthy conscience that will be a powerful motivating force in the life of individuals and groups. The emphasis should be on encouraging growth, on working with strengths rather than simply focusing on manifest problems. The total corporate life of a worshiping, learning, serving congregation can help the consciences of members and leaders to keep growing. When this happens people may perhaps be spared some of the suffering associated with the conscience problems described in this book.

Toward the end of a series of seminars for clergy on "Conscience and Pastoral Care" participants expressed the need for a constructive statement on the nature of the healthy conscience. Having read this far in *Conscience and Caring* you may feel the same need. Since conscience can be either healthy or unhealthy, either humanizing or dehumanizing, we need criteria other than those provided by conscience itself to guide us in assessing and developing our values. If conscience at its best is a call to wholeness, we need a vision of what constitutes authentic wholeness. Although the New Testament does not provide us with a developed theology of conscience, it does provide us with basic resources for constructing such a theology. For Christians, our vision of wholeness is expressed most clearly in the person of Jesus Christ.

In what follows I shall attempt to list and describe six characteristics of Christian conscience, the ideal conscience as understood psychologically in the light of Christ's life and teachings. The healthy conscience, of course, is the first to recognize that none of us ever reaches such an ideal. The ideal can nonetheless become a creative and powerful motivating force in our lives.

Liberated

The Christian conscience is first of all a liberated conscience, liberated through the acceptance and forgiveness of God that is made humanly visible and tangible in Jesus Christ. Believers are confident that God accepts them despite their continuing failure and inadequacy. The Christian conscience is liberated from the domination of guilt and the fear of rejection, from futile efforts at self-justification and abortive attempts to earn the acceptance of others by anxious striving. It is liberated from all subservience to rules and regulations, and from inner compulsion to conform to a group or to a legal code.

Paul Tillich put forward the concept of a "transmoral conscience," that is, a conscience which takes moral laws seriously but interprets them in the light of love.* A conscience that has been set free by Christ may be understood as "transmoral," having the same attitudes toward moral and religious laws that Jesus expressed. Such a conscience is predominantly positive and joyful, self-affirming rather than self-condemning. A person who is set free for caring and responsible service in the world is no longer dominated by anxious, perfectionist pressures to conform or to achieve.

The awakening of this positive, liberated conscience does not mean that negative conscience has been forever vanquished, so that a person no longer feels its power. Rather, the conscience that has been set free in Christ now has the strength and courage to face negative conscience, to bear its guilt without being dominated by it. Insofar as persons of faith share responsibility for a world full of greed, bitterness, and suffering, it is appropriate that they experience the pain of a negative conscience. This negative conscience, however, is built into and transformed by the liberated conscience which has accepted God's loving forgiveness and responded to his call to care. A liberated conscience is not to be identified directly with a clear conscience, for the latter can be and often is gained through simple sacrifice of honesty. There is a continuing tension in the life of a Christian between the joy of a liberated conscience and the pain of a sensitive, responsible conscience.

For some people the journey toward even an initial sense of liberation may be long and difficult. There is often a great deal to unlearn. Negative conscience processes, derived from early childhood, become so much a part of the personality that a prolonged experience of consistent grace through caring persons, including pastors and counselors, may be necessary to open the way for God's transforming work. Everyone's experience is different, and it can be dangerous to use the experience of others to evaluate one's own pilgrimage.

Shaped by the Koinonia

Christian conscience is shaped and developed by participation in Christian community. Conscience is social in nature. It grows through relationships, through participation in groups and in society generally. In the voice of conscience we hear and respond to the "voices" of the persons and groups with which we are associated. Though the believer participates in many communities and is inevitably influenced by them, there is one community that is crucial for the fashioning of Christian conscience—the covenant community of faith. To varying degrees the attitudes and values of the church are internalized within its members and become a motivating force in their daily living.

The church may be identified theologically as one vast community, namely the community of all those who are committed to Christ and share his mission. From a sociological point of view, however, the church is many communities, with varying beliefs and values. The true community of faith, the *koinonia*, should not be identified directly with the empirical church, but neither should the two be sharply separated. The empirical church is both faithful and unfaithful. It celebrates and responds to God's saving acts and the values bound up with these acts, but it can also fail to respond to God; it can reject Christian values. The Christian believes nonetheless that God speaks and acts through that community, and within it the human conscience can respond to God's call and become a part of God's mission. Within the *koinonia* we hear God's call to full humanity, to a life of caring and responsible service; there we experience the love and correction of fellow believers who are also responding to the call to care. The ideal is simply but beautifully expressed by Dietrich Bonhoeffer: "Jesus Christ has become my conscience."*

Pastors need to avoid becoming so involved with counseling in problem situations that they neglect constructive community building. Conscious emphasis needs to be placed on fostering the development of loving, accepting relationships, in which honest confrontation can take place without creating bitterness or hurt. Small, conscience-nurturing groups fulfill a vital role in community building. Such construction is an ongoing process, for Christian conscience never finally arrives—it is constantly being reshaped and renewed.

Continually Growing

This leads to the third characteristic of the mature, Christian conscience: it is continually growing. From the outset we have viewed conscience as a dynamic process rather than as a static state or structure. However, conscience processes can be arrested in their development. Immature superego dimensions of conscience can remain relatively unchanged from early childhood. At times, it may seem easier to live with a conscience of "black and white" absolutes. Changing one's values is often a painful process! An immature conscience, however, is maintained only through denial of reality and loss of integrity. A healthy conscience, understood as a call to full humanity and to active caring, remains open to fresh stimulation and new experience. Christian conscience should be reawakened to new growth again and again by God's gracious actions, by the vision of authentic humanity in Jesus Christ, by facing life's crises, and by discovering new areas of human need.

We have seen how conscience tends to be limited in its areas of operation, how it can be active in some areas of life and remain inactive or distorted in others. We all have our conscience blind spots, being complacent about some things which call out for our concern. Christian conscience grows through the elimination of some of these gaps, as our conscience processes become more consistent, aware, and inclusive. We all need confrontal experiences that will challenge our conscience blind spots.

There are many resources within the Christian tradition for stimulating the growth of more sensitive and concerned consciences. Over the past few years, meditation and contemplation have become more central in my own life, as indeed they have for many people. The arts of relaxation and meditation, the values of fantasy and guided imagery especially when these are linked with Bible study and prayer, the discipline of contemplation, as when centering thought and attention on some of the great words or themes of the Christian faith—all these have been enriching, uplifting, and freeing for me. I believe they bring a reawakening and strengthening of conscience processes. They are also a valuable resource in counseling.

Though I have rejected any simple equation of conscience with the voice of God, God's voice can indeed be heard through conscience, especially through a renewed, growing conscience. The more conscience is confronted by God's judgment and refashioned by God's grace, the more likely it can become a reminder and a channel of God's truth.

Integrated

The maturing healthy conscience is an integrated conscience, associated with personal wholeness. The holistic approach to conscience outlined in chapter 1 fosters wholeness. We have seen that some dimensions of conscience, especially negative or guilty dimensions, can develop their own autonomy and become separated from other conscience processes. These alienated dimensions of conscience can become powerful, producing fragmentation and conflict. In healthy Christian living, the various levels of conscience become more integrated with each other. Rational or cognitive levels, that is, our beliefs and thoughts about values, are closely linked with nonrational or emotional levels. The guiding conscience, which is focused on decision making and the future, is bound up with the judging conscience, which looks back to and learns from the past. An integrated conscience makes for consistency and integrity in living, though it is not necessarily free of conflict. At times even a person with a sensitive and responsible conscience inevitably feels pulled in different directions. The conflicts, however, can be faced realistically, worked through, and sometimes resolved, with responsible decision making and action as the outcome.

"Wholeness" is a major theme in the New Testament; it is closely related to both health and salvation. When health is understood as a growth process, involving the utilization of our abilities and gifts in creative living, the mature conscience can be interpreted as a call toward health and wholeness. As we have seen, conscience is often so much less than this— which indicates that conscience itself needs to be healed so that it can fulfill its proper functions in our lives. An integrated conscience, then, is a healed conscience, healed of destructive divisions and conflicts. This healing process should continue through all of life for no one's conscience is ever fully integrated!

Caring

The mature Christian conscience is also a caring conscience. The conscience which has been liberated by God's forgiveness and acceptance calls us to care about our neighbor. Bonhoeffer expressed it well: "The conscience which has been set free is not timid like the conscience which is bound by the law, but it stands wide open for our neighbor and for his concrete distress."*

Caring is a vague term, interpreted in various ways; it needs to be given precise meaning.† Genuine caring goes further than simply liking, or having sympathy, or wanting to help. It is not an isolated feeling or a temporary emotion called forth by pity. Caring is an authentic accepting of another person and a giving of the total self in a warm relationship. In caring, I help another person to grow and I accept help in my own growth. I am concerned about the whole person, not just about a symptom or problem.

Genuine caring does not overlook the day-to-day needs, the smile, the gesture, the handshake, the kindly deed; but neither does it forget the deeper needs and long-term goals. It does not do for others what they could better do for themselves. In caring, I make myself present and available, but I do not impose myself. Genuine caring respects privacy. It respects the boundaries of the other person's life and allows the other person space in which to move. It does not intrude into sensitive areas unless invited to do so.

Caring is patient, allowing others to move at their own pace. It is also honest, prepared to help another person face truth and reality, even when that may be hurtful. There is a mutuality in genuine caring, so that I am ready to receive my friend's caring as well as to express care for my friend. I am ready to receive graciously, as well as to give generously. Caring involves a readiness to enter another person's world, without losing touch with my own. I am ready to feel and share the despair of my friend, yet I do not lose hold of my own hope. Caring does not give way to easy optimism or wishful thinking, nor does it lose sight of the finest possibilities of the other; it does not despair of the power of love. Since caring is essentially positive and outgoing, negative conscience no longer dominates, though its voice is never completely silenced. In genuine caring, helping a neighbor in trouble is more important to me than my own need to maintain a clear conscience or good reputation. Caring breaks through the limitations of "tribal" conscience, for genuine caring knows no limits of race, nation, or religion.

Responsible

Caring is closely related to the last characteristic of Christian conscience: it is socially responsible. Caring in its broadest sense includes responsibility. If we are genuinely concerned about other human beings, we will also be concerned about the social and political structures that affect their lives so profoundly.

This century has witnessed the rapid growth in our society of multitudes of organizations and institutions. These institutions, drawing people together from widely dispersed geographical areas, develop their own unity, values, and life style. The values and attitudes developed in institutional life tend to be internalized by individual members, so that they become a part of the inner dialogue of conscience. Christian conscience has a deep sense of responsibility about such social structures, realizing that people's lives are inextricably bound up with their institutions. There needs to be a pastoral care of social structures and organizations, as well as of individuals and families.* The pastoral and prophetic ministries should not be separated, for each needs the other. Persons of mature conscience, recognizing the importance of social and political factors in the shaping of human life, do not shy away from controversial public issues. They do not stand on the sidelines as spectators offering easy answers to the problems. Instead they join the struggle to find the most constructive and human solutions possible.

A healthy, sensitive conscience calls us to global responsibility. The Christian, as a believer in the one God of all creation and in the essential oneness of the human family, is summoned to share in a total world mission that seeks fulfillment for all humankind. "The world is our parish." The Christian conscience at its best is marked by inclusiveness. No human issue is outside the range of its concern. There are no human boundaries to Christian responsibility, no acceptable divisions of people into "us" and "them." Our shared humanity binds us together, transcending the boundaries brought about by narrow, tribal consciences.

A deep sense of social responsibility makes us aware of our corporate guilt. We all share in the responsibility for the plight of humankind and for making human society more whole. While injustice and suffering remain in the world, guilt remains, and it is appropriate and healthy that we experience our due proportion of it. There is both the guilt derived from our participation in the corporate life and lot of the human family and also the guilt that comes from our personal wrong-doing. The two cannot be separated. This issue is very important for our counseling ministry. Pastors need to be aware of the danger of offering the luxury of a clear conscience, nurtured by cheap grace, in exchange for a troubled and hurting conscience. The first state could be worse than the last.

The Christian life may be interpreted as a response to God's gracious action in Jesus Christ and to God's continuing activity in the world. Our "response-ability" depends on God's prior action and continuing grace. It is when we respond in faith to God's actions that we experience God's enabling power. Faith becomes the link between the call of conscience and the life of discipleship. It helps to generate the courage we need if we are to take the risks involved in responding to the call of conscience to become more human.

As we endeavor to help others in their struggles with conscience, we should not lose our vision of what the human conscience can become when inspired by the dynamic of a growing faith. The liberation that comes through the experience of God's grace within the community of faith helps conscience to become more constructive and integrated, more caring and responsible. If this vision of the maturing healthy conscience becomes powerful for us and for those with whom we counsel, our counseling will have achieved one of its important goals.

Notes

Page
3. *See Wright, *The Psychology of Moral Behavior,* pp. 28–30, for a brief discussion of the nature of conscience from a psychological point of view.
4. *Ibid., pp. 38–43.
5. *Ina Corinne Brown, *Understanding Other Cultures* (Englewood Cliffs, N.J.: Spectrum, 1963), p. 106.
5. †Ibid., p. 95.
5. ‡Tillich, *Morality and Beyond,* p. 65.
6. *See Pierce, *Conscience in the New Testament,* esp. chaps. 4 and 6.
6. †Sigmund Freud also wrote about the formation of positive conscience, which he called the "ego ideal," but this aspect of his thought remained relatively undeveloped. His use of the terms "conscience," "ego ideal," and "superego" was not always consistent. See *New Introductory Lectures in Psycho-Analysis* (London: Hogarth, 1962), pp. 78–106.
6. ‡Quoted in Pierce, *Conscience,* p. 48.
6. §See, for example, Lehmann, *Ethics in a Christian Context,* pp. 330–32.
6. ‖For an outline of the research of Piaget and Kohlberg, see Duska and Whelan, *Moral Development,* chaps. 1 and 2.
7. *John Macquarrie, "The Struggle of Conscience for Authentic Selfhood," in *Conscience: Theological and Psychological Perspectives,* ed. Nelson, p. 156.
8. *For a discussion of the social theory of conscience, see H. Richard Niebuhr, *The Responsible Self* (New York: Harper & Row, 1963), pp. 75–79.
8. †See Emile Durkheim, *Moral Education* (New York: The

Page

Free Press of Glencoe, 1973), pp. 59–79; and *Suicide: A Study in Sociology* (London: Routledge & Kegan Paul, 1970), p. 318.

9. *See Martin Heidegger, *Being and Time* (New York: Harper & Row, 1962), pp. 313–418; and Martin Buber, "Guilt and Guilt Feelings," in *Conscience,* ed. Nelson, pp. 224–37.

10. *For Rousseau's views of conscience, see Edward Engelberg, *The Unknown Distance: From Consciousness to Conscience* (Cambridge: Harvard University Press, 1972), p. 24. For Newman, see, for example, Americo D. Lapati, *John Henry Newman* (New York: Twayne, 1972), pp. 113, 114.

10. †Even Catholic scholars with a lofty view of conscience affirm its fallibility. See, for example, Bernhard Häring, *The Law of Christ,* vol. 1 (Westminster: Newman, 1966), pp. 154–57.

13. *Bull, *Moral Judgment from Childhood to Adolescence,* p. 60.

13. †Helen Lynd, *On Shame and the Search for Identity* (New York: Harcourt, Brace & Co., 1958), p. 49.

13. ‡See, for example, James N. Lapsley, "A Psycho-Theological Appraisal of the New Left," *Theology Today* 25:4 (January 1969): 446–61.

16. *See Howard W. Stone, *Using Behavioral Methods in Pastoral Counseling* (Philadelphia: Fortress, 1980) for a description of methods of relaxation that can be helpful in pastoral counseling.

17. *Freud, *New Introductory Lectures,* p. 83.

18. *Ibid., p. 85.

18. †For constructive ways of rechanneling anger, see David W. Augsburger, *Anger and Assertiveness in Pastoral Care* (Philadelphia: Fortress, 1979).

18. ‡Martin Luther, *Luther's Works,* vol. 7, ed. Jaroslov Pelikan (St. Louis: Concordia, 1964), p. 290.

21. *Menninger, *Whatever Became of Sin?* p. 84.

21. †See William Clebsch and Clifford Jaekle, *Pastoral Care in Historical Perspective* (Englewood Cliffs, N.J.: Prentice-Hall, 1964), pp. 294–308.

21. ‡Macquarrie, "Struggle of Conscience," p. 156.

22. *A. Beisser, "The Paradoxical Theory of Change," in *Gestalt*

Page

Therapy Now: Theory, Techniques, Applications, ed. Joen Fagan and Irma L. Shepherd (New York: Harper & Row, 1971), pp. 77–80.

22. †For appropriate methods of making referrals, see William Oglesby, *Referral in Pastoral Counseling* (Philadelphia: Fortress, 1969), esp. chap. 3.

23. *For a more detailed description of this exercise, and for other similar exercises, see John O. Stevens, *Awareness: Exploring, Experimenting, Experiencing* (New York: Bantam, 1971), pp. 68–70, 175, 176.

25. *John Glaser, "Conscience and Superego: A Key Distinction," in *Conscience,* ed. Nelson, p. 182.

26. *Many studies have indicated that masturbation is indeed widespread among both men and women. It can fulfill a constructive role for some people, especially during times of sexual deprivation. Yet many fallacious, guilty fears still center around the practice. See James B. Nelson, *Embodiment: An Approach to Sexuality and Christian Theology* (Minneapolis: Augsburg, 1978), pp. 168–73.

26. †Erikson, *Insight and Responsibility,* p. 145. He is quoting Julian Huxley.

26. ‡Erich Fromm, *Man for Himself* (London: Routledge & Kegan Paul, 1960), pp. 141–72.

27. *Gerard Egan, *The Skilled Helper* (Monterey: Brooks/Cole, 1975), pp. 151–55.

32. *From Hobart O. Mowrer's Foreword to William Glasser, *Reality Therapy: A New Approach to Psychiatry* (New York: Harper & Row, 1965), p. xiii.

32. †Stein, *Guilt: Theory and Therapy,* pp. 143, 144.

33. *Glasser, *Reality Therapy,* esp. part 1.

33. †See, for example, Browning, *Moral Context*; and Hoffman, *Ethical Confrontation.*

34. *Hoffman, *Ethical Confrontation,* p. 3.

34. †See Knight, *Conscience and Guilt,* pp. 129, 130.

35. *For an introduction to family pastoral care methods, see Howard Clinebell, *Basic Types of Pastoral Counseling* (Nashville: Abingdon, 1966), chap. 7; Charles W. Stewart, *The Minister as Family Counselor* (Nashville: Abingdon, 1979);

Page

and Douglas A. Anderson, *New Approaches to Family Pastoral Care* (Philadelphia: Fortress, 1980).

37. *Carl Jung, "A Psychological View of Conscience," in *Conscience*, ed. Curatorium of the C. G. Jung Institute, p. 182.

37. †Some of these stories are found in Duska and Whelan, *Moral Development*, pp. 115–23. See also Peter Scharf, ed., *Readings in Moral Education* (Minneapolis: Winston, 1978), esp. pp. 62–81.

39. *Duska and Whelan, *Moral Development*, p. 121.

39. †Viktor Frankl, *Man's Search for Meaning: An Introduction to Logotherapy* (Boston: Beacon, 1962).

42. *Abraham Maslow, *Religions, Values and Peak Experiences* (New York: Viking, 1970), p. 83.

43. *Allen Wheelis, *The Quest for Identity* (New York: W. W. Norton, 1958), pp. 97–103.

48. *See Matthew 4:1–11 and Luke 4:1–13.

49. *Carl Rogers, *Freedom to Learn* (Columbus, Oh.: Charles E. Merrill, 1969), p. 241.

52. *See, for example, Irving Polster and Miriam Polster, *Gestalt Therapy Integrated: Contours of Theory and Practice* (New York: Vintage, 1974), p. 265–269.

52. †Maslow, *Religions,* p. 19.

56. *Proverbs 31:10–31.

57. *Erikson, *Insight,* p. 145.

57. †Luke 18:11, 12.

60. *Luke 18:18–30.

60. †See Thomas Gordon, *P.E.T.: Parent Effectiveness Training* (New York, Wydon, 1972), chaps. 6 and 7, for a discussion of "you messages" and "I messages."

62. *Carl Jung et al., *Man and His Symbols* (New York: Dell, 1972), p. 17.

62. †Viktor Frankl, *The Unconscious God* (New York: Simon & Schuster, 1975), p. 41.

63. *For a good presentation of Jung's concept of "the shadow," see Erich Neumann, *Depth Psychology and a New Ethic* (New York: Harper & Row, 1973), chap. IV and the Appendix.

64. *Mark 10:13–23.

64. †Matthew 18:3.

64. ‡See, for example, Eric Berne, *Games People Play* (London: Andre Deutsch, 1966) and *Transactional Analysis in Psychotherapy* (New York: Grove, 1961); and Muriel James and Dorothy Jongeward, *Born to Win* (Reading, Mass.: Addison-Wesley, 1971), esp. chap. 6.

65. *Frederick Perls et al., *Gestalt Therapy: Excitement and Growth in the Human Personality* (New York: Delta, 1951), p. 297.

65. †See Berne, *Transactional Analysis,* pp. 224–31.

68. *Tillich, *Morality and Beyond,* pp. 65–81.

70. *Bonhoeffer, *Ethics,* p. 244.

72. *Ibid.

72. †In what follows I have been influenced by Mayeroff, *On Caring.*

74. *See, for example, the articles by R. Bonthius and Don Browning in Howard Clinebell, ed., *Community Mental Health: The Role of Church and Temple* (Nashville: Abingdon, 1970), pp. 41–46 and 110–18 respectively. See also Speed Leas and Paul Kittlaus, *The Pastoral Counselor in Social Action* (Philadelphia: Fortress, 1981).

Annotated Bibliography

Allison, C. Fitzsimons. *Guilt, Anger and God*. New York: Seabury, 1972. Deals with the destructive effects of guilt, anger, and the fear of death, and presents the response of the gospel.

Becker, Arthur H. *Guilt: Curse or Blessing?* Minneapolis: Augsburg, 1977. A clinically trained pastor argues that guilt has its positive aspects and can be creative rather than destructive.

Bier, William C., ed. *Conscience: Its Freedom and Limitations*. New York: Fordham University Press, 1971. A series of articles, mainly by Catholic scholars, on the nature of conscience, especially as it relates to human freedom.

Bonhoeffer, Dietrich. *Ethics*. London: Collins, 1964. This classic in theological ethics includes theological treatments of conscience and guilt.

Browning, Don S. *The Moral Context of Pastoral Care*. Philadelphia: Westminster, 1976. Argues that pastoral care should be exercised within a context of moral meanings and explores ways of fostering a growing awareness of those meanings.

Bull, Norman. *Moral Judgment from Childhood to Adolescence*. Beverly Hills, Ca.: Sage, 1969. Reports an extensive English survey on moral development in children and adolescents.

Clinebell, Charlotte H. *Counseling for Liberation*. Philadelphia: Fortress, 1976. Presents methods for linking counseling with consciousness-raising.

Clinebell, Howard J. *Growth Counseling for Mid-Years Couples*. Philadelphia: Fortress, 1977. A practical guide for pastors counseling married couples in their middle years; includes helpful methods for revising values.

————. *Growth Groups: Marriage and Family Enrichment, Creative Singlehood, Human Liberation, Youth Work, Social Change*. Nashville: Abingdon, 1977. Gives principles and methods for leading growth groups, many of which are concerned with value issues.

The Curatorium of the C. G. Jung Institute, ed. *Conscience.* Evanston, Ill.: Northwestern University Press, 1970. A series of articles on the concept of conscience by Jungian scholars, with one by Jung himself.

Curran, Charles. *Religious Values in Counseling and Psychotherapy.* New York: Sheed & Ward, 1969. Discusses questions of sin, guilt, and anxiety, and the place of confession in personal counseling.

Daly, Mary. *Beyond God the Father: Toward a Philosophy of Women's Liberation.* Boston: Beacon, 1974. Chapter 4 discusses oppressive masculine ethics and the contribution of feminist ethics to an understanding of true morality.

Duska, Roland, and Whelan, Mariellen. *Moral Development: A Guide to Piaget and Kohlberg.* New York: Paulist, 1975. An introduction to the theories of Piaget and Kohlberg on moral development, with discussion of the implications for Christian morality and educational practice.

Erikson, Erik H. *Insight and Responsibility.* New York: W. W. Norton, 1964. A collection of six lectures dealing with some of the ethical implications of psychoanalytic insights into human development.

Evans, Robert et al. *Casebook for Christian Living: Value Formation for Families and Congregations.* Atlanta: John Knox, 1977. Presents twelve case studies that raise value issues; suitable for use in local parishes.

Graham, Douglas. *Moral Learning and Development: Theory and Research.* New York: Wiley and Sons, 1972. A comprehensive treatment of moral learning and development by an English psychologist, with discussion of relevant research.

Hall, Brian P. *Value Clarification as Learning Process.* 3 vols. New York: Paulist, 1973. Deals with the theory of values clarification and gives many practical exercises on values; suitable for use in Christian education and in counseling.

Hoffman, John C. *Ethical Confrontation in Counseling.* Chicago: University of Chicago Press, 1979. Argues that the nature of the healing process demands both acceptance and ethical confrontation, and appeals for a consistent moral witness in counseling.

Knight, James A. *Conscience and Guilt.* New York: Appleton-Century-Crofts, 1969. Drawing from his own clinical experience, a psychiatrist looks at some of the problems arising from an unhealthy conscience and destructive guilt.

Larson, Roland, and Larson, Doris. *Values and Faith.* Minneapolis: Winston, 1976. Contains exercises in values clarification for church groups and families.

Lehmann, Paul. *Ethics in a Christian Context.* New York: Harper & Row, 1963. The last section of this book gives a theological and historical treatment of the question of conscience.

Mayeroff, Milton. *On Caring.* New York: Harper & Row, 1973. A helpful philosophical discussion of caring and loving relationships.

Menninger, Karl. *Whatever Became of Sin?* New York: Hawthorn, 1975. A vigorous critique by a distinguished psychiatrist of current attitudes towards "sin," and of current social practices.

Miller, Donald E. *The Wing-Footed Wanderer: Conscience and Transcendence.* Nashville: Abingdon, 1977. Draws together psychological, philosophical, and theological considerations in discussing the nature of conscience and the processes of moral development.

Mount, Eric. *Conscience and Responsibility.* Richmond: John Knox, 1969. A study in theological ethics that links conscience with community and interprets it as the call to social responsibility.

Mowrer, O. Hobart, ed. *Morality and Mental Health.* Chicago: Rand McNally & Co., 1967. A collection of articles that raise a wide range of moral issues in psychiatry, therapy, and pastoral care.

Nelson, C. Ellis, ed. *Conscience: Theological and Psychological Perspectives.* New York: Newman, 1973. A collection of twenty-two articles on the nature of conscience from theological and psychological perspectives.

Pierce, Claude A. *Conscience in the New Testament.* London: SCM, 1955. A study of the meanings of the term "conscience" in the writings of the New Testament.

Simon, Sidney B. *Meeting Yourself Halfway.* Niles, Ill.: Argus, 1974. Contains thirty-one values clarification strategies helpful for daily living.

Stein, Edward V. *Guilt: Theory and Therapy.* Philadelphia: West-minster, 1968. A comprehensive treatment of the nature of guilt and its development, from psychological and sociological per-spectives, and a discussion of the healing that comes from a "religion of love."

Stephenson, Geoffrey M. *The Development of Conscience.* New York: Humanities, 1966. The report of an English study of psychopathic youths and its implications for our understanding of the development of conscience.

Tillich, Paul. *Morality and Beyond.* New York: Harper & Row, 1963. Explores the nature of conscience from a theological per-spective and presents the concept of "the transmoral con-science."

Tournier, Paul. *Guilt and Grace.* New York: Harper & Row, 1962. Discusses both true and false guilt, with frequent reference to both biblical and clinical material.

Wright, Derek. *The Psychology of Moral Behavior.* London: Pen-guin, 1976. A comprehensive treatment of psychological ap-proaches to moral behavior, with special attention to the results of empirical studies.